The History of the

REBEL
YELL

The History of the
REBEL
YELL

By Terryl W. Elliott

PELICAN PUBLISHING COMPANY
GRETNA 2013

First Pelican edition, 2013

Library of Congress Cataloging-in-Publication Data

Elliott, Terryl W.
  The history of the rebel yell / Terryl W. Elliott. — First Pelican edition.
    pages cm
  Includes bibliographical references and index.
  ISBN 978-1-4556-1780-7 (pbk. : alk. paper) — ISBN 978-1-4556-1794-4 (e-book)
  1. United States—History—Civil War, 1861-1865—Miscellanea. 2. Confederate
States of America. Army—Miscellanea. 3. Battle-cries. I. Title.
  E468.9.E55 2013
  973.7--dc23
                                2012043545

Printed in the United States of America
Published by Pelican Publishing Company, Inc.
1000 Burmaster Street, Gretna, Louisiana 70053

To the memory of my grandfather,
Charles M. Rockwood,
who first instilled in me a lifelong love of history

CONTENTS

ACKNOWLEDGMENTS

I would like to thank my friend and fellow historian, Harold Dellinger, who had a major role in the conception of this project. His interest in the Rebel Yell sparked my own, and his encouragement during the writing of this book helped keep it moving.

I would also like to thank another friend, Vicki Beck, who has been helpful to me in many ways through the years. She had the good sense to remind me that the important thing about writing was to continue to enjoy it.

I also want to recognize the researchers and historians whose previous work on the Rebel Yell served as a foundation on which I was able to build. I especially wish to thank Monte Akers (historian, author and friend), S. Waite Rawls III and John Coski of the Museum of the Confederacy, and authors Clint Johnson and Steve Cottrell for the valuable time they gave me in discussing various aspects of the subject.

Finally, I want to give thanks to my wife, "Sam," who always supports and never complains.

INTRODUCTION

Among the countless subjects that make up the lore and legend of the Civil War there is perhaps none more iconic than the myth and mystery surrounding the Confederate battle cry—the famous Rebel Yell.

The iconic nature of the Yell has led to its being hijacked for commercial purposes for everything from a line of casual clothing and a brand of Kentucky bourbon, to a famous rock anthem, as well as many other uses.

The most obvious statement that can be made about the Rebel Yell is that no one alive today truly knows how it sounded. While there have been numerous attempts to duplicate it—some quite well done—by re-enactors, filmmakers and others, it still remains, at best, an educated guess based on available evidence. The reliability of that evidence varies considerably depending upon its source and nature.

The sources range from writers, historians and others over the last seventy-five years or so, to first hand accounts from soldiers at the time, as well as recollections from veterans years later. There is even a small amount of recorded sound evidence that is extremely enticing at the very least.—The nature of the evidence ranges from the apocryphal and/or anecdotal to the descriptive and the phonetic. There is also a considerable amount of information concerning background, origin and variation.

The intent of this book is to present as much of the available evidence as possible in an orderly, readable and enjoyable manner; and to then sort through the accumulated material and draw some conclusions.

I will be acting as a "guide" to the reader as we search for, and investigate, the Rebel Yell, which admittedly gives me the opportunity to insert some of my own thoughts and interpretations about any specific subject being looked at during our investigation. Hopefully this will help "lighten the load" a bit, because the most important thing for readers of history is to enjoy themselves, while digging a little deeper into a subject than they have in the past....So relax, take a deep breath and get ready to Yell!

The History of the

REBEL YELL

PART I: ORIGINS

CHAPTER 1

Prologue: A Bit of Background

There has to be a starting point and this one is as good as any: During battle soldiers and warriors have always screamed, shouted, hollered and yelled! There are examples of this throughout recorded history, and no doubt in pre-history as well.—Certainly cavemen, whether Neanderthal or Cro-Magnon, must have hollered their guts out as they swung clubs and threw spears at the enemy, as well as at available meat sources. (We can only hope that these two targets didn't coincide with one another too often!)—In some instances this activity was undoubtedly planned as part of an army's overall battle strategy. But it occurred just as often, if not more so, due to the pure adrenaline rush of battle.

Whether it was intentionally planned strategy or an instinctual, gut-level phenomenon, the battle cry had two primary purposes: First, was to unnerve and frighten the enemy, making their response to attack less effective and possibly causing retreat. Second, was to keep that valuable, and much needed, adrenaline pumping in order to help the attacking force overcome its own fear of battle.

Through the years the forms that this shouting has taken have varied dramatically. There have been highly formalized cheers—often accompanied by martial music in some form. Think here of the British regulars entering battle in the late Eighteenth and early Nineteenth Centuries while in formation with drums beating cadence and unit "huzzahs" filling the air. On the other end of the spectrum would be the war cry of the African tribesman or the war whoop of the Native American warrior; certainly less formalized, but no less effective—possibly more so! Of course, there is a wide spectrum between these two extremes.

As a general statement it can be said that during the American Civil War the Federal troops more closely followed the British example, while the Confederate Army's yell was much more akin to the "savage" screams of the various native tribes. In truth, both fall somewhere in between on the overall spectrum.

The Rebel Yell was renowned throughout the world even before the War was over, when it slipped into the realm of historical legend. Its uniqueness and its demoralizing effect, which is said to have caused enemy soldiers to flee merely upon hearing it, were the basis for this fame.

Because of its popularity Confederate troops worked at becoming a "good yelling unit" or maybe the "best yelling regiment," or achieving some other acclaim for their ability to deliver the Yell.—Their reward for this skill was often an assignment to be deployed as advance forces at the beginning of a battle in order that the Rebel Yell could do its damage, including giving the Federals the impression of the Southerners having a much larger force than they actually possessed (see chapter 15). This was particularly true during the first year or so of the Civil War when the South was heavily outnumbered, outgunned and out supplied, unlike later years, when these problems rose to outrageously ludicrous proportions.

The Rebel Yell, while primarily employed during charges or in celebration following a victory, had other uses as well. It was passed along the columns while on the march and passed around from unit to unit in camp. This was similar to "the wave" being passed around a modern sports stadium and had the same basic purpose—to lift morale and inspire enthusiasm. It was even said to be used as a wake-up call in the morning.

Is it any wonder that the Rebel Yell has been called "as much a part of a Rebel's fighting equipment as his musket"?

In order not to over simplify our search for the Rebel Yell—after all, where's the fun in that?—we now need to dig a little deeper, and in more detail, into some British and American history. Trust me...it's necessary!

Other than the institution of slavery, the Celtic people who emigrated from the British Isles were the single greatest influence on the culture of the South by the time of the Civil War. This theory of Southern folkways has been expounded most regularly by professor and author, Grady McWhiney, in numerous books and articles. It is a theory I advocate, and which plays a prominent role in our subject, because this Southern-Celtic culture was also the incubator for what became the Rebel Yell. So, it's important to understand their history—where they came from, their lifestyle and politics, what they had to endure through the years, why they came to America and what they did when they got here. The largest and most influential of these Celtic groups were the Scots-Irish, so we'll begin with them.

CHAPTER 2

The Scots-Irish Influence—Great Britain: Border Reivers and Woodkernes

To understand and appreciate one primary component of the Rebel Yell we need to understand an ethnic group of people known in America as the Scots-Irish (also: Scotch-Irish). Their long history of violent encounters, their migratory lifestyle, the topography of the land where they lived, their language and other means of communication, their religion, loyalties and belief systems all led to their location and situation at the start of the Civil War, and their singular contribution to the nature of the Rebel Yell.—Like many searches for information, this one is more complex than it seems on the surface.

There had long been a cross migration between the islands of Britain and Ireland. Indeed it was Gaels from Ireland who originally colonized parts of Scotland and over time drove out the existing Pictish culture. The Gaels were called Scoti by the Romans and eventually the name stuck to both the people and the country.

Scotland is geographically divided in three sections: The first is the Highlands, comprised of the Northwest Highlands, the Grampian Mountains and the Islands of the North Sea. This is where the traditional Catholic, Gaelic speaking tribal clans held out against the Protestant, English government for so long. The second is the Central Lowlands, which is fairly self-explanatory; made up largely of peat bogs, marshes and moors. Finally, there is the Southern Uplands (or Border Country) which can best be described as low rolling hills that blend in with the Northern English border country along the River Tweed. These last two sections are jointly referred to as Lowland Scotland (or just

the Lowlands, as opposed to the Highlands). The Lowland
Scots were an amalgam of the Scoti/Gaels, remnants of the
Picts, various Scandinavian Viking groups, native Britons
and Anglo-Saxons. These Lowland Scots were different in
language, culture and ultimately in religion from the Gaelic
inhabitants of the Highlands and the Islands. It is the
Lowland Scots—along with some of their English border
neighbors—that make their way to the frontier of Northern
Ireland, a land not unlike the uplands, and vastly better
than the lowlands of Scotland.

In 1603 Elizabeth I, the last Tudor monarch, had been
replaced by James VI of Scotland, who also became James I
of England and Ireland. In the same year the Earl of Tyrone,
chief of the O'Neill clan, and the Earl of Tyrconnell, chief of
the O'Donnell clan, the two leading families in the province
of Ulster, surrendered to the English. While the rest of
Ireland had been yoked by the English earlier, Ulster had
been the last stronghold of the Irish; it was here they made
their final stand. The fighting was exceptionally bitter and
brutal; not only were Irishmen and Englishmen battling,
but Catholics were struggling against Protestants. After the
surrender, Ulster was a scene of total devastation, and the
people were completely demoralized. Despite this situation,
the English still had only marginal control over Ireland
and were looking for ways to gain stability and rebuild the
Ulster wasteland.

Shortly thereafter James authorized a private enterprise
to colonize and replenish the depopulated counties of Ulster.
The concept was to be carried out almost exclusively by
Lowland Scots, along with a few Border English to further
strengthen the fact that Ireland was an English possession.
This allowed James to gain a Lowland Scot, Protestant and
English speaking foothold in Gaelic speaking, Catholic
Ireland. There was little trouble finding Lowlanders ready
to start new lives in Ulster, even though the task they found
there was indeed daunting. However, the land was good
and relatively unfarmed as the Irish had used it more for
pasturing rather than tilling; and the new settlers could

get more land with longer leases than in Scotland. As the colony gained success more and more Scots poured across the North Channel in search of land.

In 1607, following the initial success of the private enterprise colony, James found himself with an ideal opportunity to further expand his hold on Ulster. The Earls of both the O'Neills and O'Donnells fled to the continent. They had suffered harassment and abuse at the hands of the English following their surrender, and by 1607 they feared for their safety. This left James with huge tracts of land (approximately 3.8 million acres) which he now had control over.

To further the aims and success of the earlier colony, James now created a Crown sponsored venture that came to be known as the Ulster Plantation. Tracts of land were granted to men called "undertakers" (Protestant Scots or English) and "servitors" (military or government personnel) who in turn leased and rented out parcels of land to new settlers. Once again the vast majority of the migrants were Lowland Scots, although this wave, which was in full force by 1610, included more Border English than the first settlement. The resettlement of the Lowland Scots and the Border English to the Ulster Plantation solved two problems for James; he was able to repopulate Ulster with mostly Protestant Scots—although they were Calvinist Presbyterians instead of Anglicans—and he helped solve the problem of the troublesome "Border Reivers"—both Scots and English—who kept the area in constant turmoil. Better to send them to Ulster and fight the Irish Catholics instead of each other! By 1619 there were over 8,000 families of Scots living in Ulster.

The native Irish chieftains who remained in Northern Ireland were forced to go into the hills; where, operating as guerillas, they harassed and attacked the new settlers with hit-and-run tactics. These "outlaws" were known as "Woodkernes" (also: Widkairns), a term that translates as "wood fighters."

To anyone who is familiar with the Border War and the Civil War on the Missouri-Kansas border, the names and tactics of the Border Reivers of Scotland and England, the Woodkernes of Ireland and similar groups in the Scottish Highlands called "Mosstroopers" should have a very authentic ring. Think here of "Border Ruffians" and "Bushwhackers," similarly named "outlaw" groups using the same guerilla-style tactics.

Eventually, the same solution and result occurred in Northern Ireland that took place during and after the Civil War two centuries later. The English government evicted all civilians from areas where the guerillas operated, and sold those who refused to surrender into indentured servitude. This is almost identical to the infamous Order No. 11 which depopulated all or parts of four Missouri border counties for their support of guerilla fighters such as William Quantrill.

After various wars these Celtic guerillas invariably turned the focus of their activities to outright crime just as the James-Younger gang did after the Civil War. The term "social bandit" has been defined as an outlaw who is not regarded as a criminal by his own extended community. Following in the footsteps of Robin Hood, these early Celtic outlaws are considered to be among the first social bandits, a title their nineteenth-century American counterparts would inherit.

Life was tough in Ulster for the Scots settlers, but they had an undeniable hardiness, brought about by years of deprivation and fighting against the English, which pulled them through and made the Plantation relatively prosperous. Besides the livestock and farm crops, their lives were helped tremendously by the lowly potato, which was a recent arrival from America. They further supplemented their livelihood with wild game and with bounties paid for killing both wolves and Woodkernes. (The parallels that can be drawn comparing what they faced in Ulster with what was waiting for them in the wilds of the North American frontier, among the Native Americans, are unmistakable.)

The primary point to be made here, in relation to our

study of the Rebel Yell, is that the Ulster Scots were the result of generations of fighting, hardscrabble farmers who brought all their past, poverty stricken, warlike ways with them when they finally made their way to America. Among those warlike ways were the various battle cries of their ancestors, going far back in Britain's history. As noted above, historically the Lowland Scots who went to Ulster were made up of many different races of people, but all from warrior tribes, and all with their own versions of war cries which were handed down, and changed and merged through the centuries to form new variations which eventually took their place as part of the tradition of the Rebel Yell.

By 1640 there were 100,000 Scots and 20,000 English in the Ulster Plantation. Calvinism, in the form of Presbyterianism and Puritanism, had taken root in Northern Ireland; but the political power still lay with the English-Anglican overseers of Ireland, and the strength of population was firmly on the side of the native Irish Catholics.

In the mid-seventeenth century, from 1641 to 1653, the two islands were consumed by war. There was civil war in England and Scotland; then the Irish rebelled when both countries attempted to assert control over Ireland. This second series of conflicts was known as the Irish Confederate Wars; they concluded with the victory over the rebels by the Lord Protector of the new Commonwealth, Oliver Cromwell.

The Plantation survived, but was badly depleted in every respect. During this period migration to Ulster had come to a halt, except for the Scots soldiers who came over to take part in the war. After the conclusion of the war some of these soldiers stayed on as settlers. From 1653 forward migration gradually resumed, and in 1660 it increased further due to new restrictions and privations being suffered in Scotland. This new wave into Ulster also included Quakers and Puritans from Wales and Northern England; later in 1685 French Huguenots began to arrive. These groups banded together with the Scots Presbyterians to form a united enclave of Protestant "dissenters" which set itself up against the other two dominant forces in Ireland, the English Anglicans and the Irish Catholics. They viewed themselves as "Ulstermen" or "Northern Irish," not Scots, English or Welsh. Certainly they were not being called Scots-Irish yet, but a new, collective, cultural identity was beginning to surface.

In spite of the resumed flow of migrants to Ulster, still more settlers were needed to overcome depopulation and the other ravages of war. But the end of the Commonwealth in 1660, and the reestablishment of the Stuart monarchy, did little to settle the unrest in the kingdom; so migration remained at a low level through 1688 when James II—a Catholic at heart—was deposed and exiled to France. Then a year later it came to a total halt, as once again, war broke out.

When James II was deposed, William of Orange and his wife, Mary—both Protestant claimants to the British throne from Holland—jointly took the throne as William III and Mary II. In 1689 James II, with a small army of French Catholic supporters, returned from the continent to Ireland. His intentions were to raise an army of Irish Catholics to join his cause and regain the British Crown. William brought an army of English and Dutch to Ireland to end the uprising. In spite of their history of being mistreated by, and battling with, the English, the majority of the Ulster Scots sided with William—he was, after all, a Protestant, albeit an Anglican one—because they could not, under any conditions, bring themselves to do anything except side against the Irish Catholics. (This, of course, is still at the core of "the troubles" in Northern Ireland to this very day.—The old adage is true: "The more things change, the more they stay the same!")

A turn of phrase, which ultimately played a significant role for the Ulster Scots from their arrival in America until the present day, had its origins in this conflict.—Because of their loyalty to William, they were sometimes referred to as "Billy Boys" by the Southern Irish Catholics. Given the hilly topography they called home, this was at some point converted into "Hill-Billies." That name would be reapplied to them by the British soldiers stationed in America, particularly as the Ulster Scots—now sometimes called Scotch-Irish—began moving into the Appalachian Mountains and pushing the frontier further west.

Once again, we find another ingredient of the Rebel Yell, this time hiding in the disparaging appellation, "Hillbillies." These soon-to-be Scots-Irish had indeed spent generations living a rural existence separated from each other by considerable distances—both those living in the true Lowlands and in the Upland Border regions. As noted above, when they came to Ulster, it was rural and hilly; and once in America they rapidly found themselves in the mountains and hills of Appalachia and the Western frontier. In all these situations a major method of communication was shouting, yelling and hollering over long distances. The most common envisioning of this mode would be someone yelling from their hilltop to a neighbor on another hilltop by way of the sound echoing through the valley between them. This tendency toward long distance hollering, in all its variations, undoubtedly became an additional part of the Scots-Irish contribution to the Yell.

Finally, in 1690 at the Battle of the Boyne, William defeated the Jacobites (as the pro-James, Catholic faction was called) in the decisive battle of the conflict. After further victories by the Williamite forces in 1691, the hostilities ceased and there was peace again in Ulster and the rest of Ireland.

Under William and Mary's rule the loyal Ulster Scots found their lot somewhat improved, but they still lacked the religious and political freedom they sought. This situation deteriorated over time, especially later, during the reign of Queen Anne when the Presbyterian Scots found themselves just as outcast as their defeated and hated Irish Catholic neighbors.

Even so, when the call went out again for new settlers roughly 50,000 more Scots came to Ulster during the final decade of the Seventeenth Century. They came to escape

high rents and famine in Scotland and take advantage of
the twenty-year leases being offered as bait.—This last
wave of migrants ultimately became the most significant
as far as the future of the Scots-Irish in America and the
Rebel Yell.

CHAPTER 3

The Scots-Irish Influence—
America: Cohees and Whiskey Boys

Their years of hardship in both Scotland and Ulster had made the future Scots-Irish a battle hardened and self reliant people, who had developed an "us-against-the-world" attitude toward others and their surroundings. One unknown writer said, "They learned from hard experience that one must fight for what he has; that turning the other cheek does not guarantee property rights; in short, that might makes right, at least in the matter of life and land ownership."

The flow of emigrants across the Atlantic had been going on since before the end of the Seventeenth Century and continued through the first decade of the 1700s. It was a relatively small number compared with what was to follow, but it represents the first wave from Ulster to America.

Several events occurred during the next decade that sped up the emigration considerably. Beginning in 1710 the various farm leases that had been granted at the end of the Jacobite Revolution started to expire. The noble landlords, whether English or Scots, refused to renew the leases without large increases in rent, sometimes double or triple the earlier rate. This began a more substantial emigrant flow to America, and then the final catalyst came in the form of a drought in 1714, which released, what was by 1717, a deluge.

There was an established flax and linen trade between Ireland and the English colonies in America; this meant that there were frequent and regular sailings across the Atlantic. A convenient means of transportation was thus available, and rather than try to exist under the current conditions, the Ulster Scots began to take advantage of it. Many times, not only large groups, but whole communities—often led by Covenanter ministers—took their leave of Northern Ireland and shipped for America.

In the years from 1717 to 1750 thousands upon thousands crossed the Atlantic from Ulster to America in a manner, and numbers, similar to their ancestors, who had crossed the North Channel over a hundred years earlier. For the next two decades a renewed economic stability in Ulster slowed the flood of emigrants to a trickle. However, in 1771 a new round of rent increases from the greedy landlords once again opened the flood gates to a new wave of emigration. In the remaining four years before the start of the American Revolution approximately 30,000 additional Ulster Scots came to the colonies; in joining those already here, they swelled the ranks of the future Scots-Irish to 250,000. While the Ulster Protestants had displayed loyalty to the crown under William of Orange, by the time they arrived in America—especially the most recent emigrants in the 1770s—they had developed a strong dislike for everything British.

The English and Scottish colonists already settled in America used the most appropriate name they had for the new arrivals from Ireland, simply calling them "Irish." These colonists were primarily of Puritan and Quaker stock, so the Ulster emigrants, not wanting to be confused for Irish Catholics by their fellow Protestants, began referring to themselves as "Scots," "Ulstermen" and "Irish Presbyterians."—While there are literary references to the "Scotch-Irish" as early as 1744, the term grew rather slowly in usage over a number of decades, culminating in the 1840s when it became a universal and common designation. During that decade, the influx of German emigrants escaping civil war at home, and the native Irish fleeing the potato famine in droves created a need for differentiation among cultural groups, particularly where the Scots-Irish and the Irish were concerned.—So, by the Civil War the Scots-Irish had an established and recognized identity.

The importance of the Scots-Irish is clearly noted in the notorious Reconstruction era novel *The Clansman*. The author, Thomas Dixon, Jr., places most of the action in the fictional Ulster County, South Carolina, and, in spite of his book's many shortcomings, proceeds to describe an interesting and accurate history of the area:

> It was settled by the Scotch folk who came from the North of Ireland in the great migrations which gave America three hundred thousand people of Covenanter martyr blood, the largest and most important addition to our population, larger in number than either the Puritans of New England or the so-called Cavaliers of Virginia and Eastern Carolina; and far more important than either, in the growth of American nationality.
>
> To a man they hated Great Britain. Not a Tory was found among them...The fiery words of Patrick Henry, their spokesman in the valley of Virginia, had swept the aristocracy of the Old Dominion into rebellion against the King and on into triumphant Democracy.
>
> They grew to the soil wherever they stopped, always home lovers and home builders, loyal to their own people, instinctive clan leaders and clan followers. A sturdy, honest, covenant-keeping, God-fearing, fighting people, above all things they hated sham and pretence. They never boasted of their families, though some of them might have quartered the royal arms of Scotland on their shields.
>
> To these sturdy qualities had been added a strain of Huguenot tenderness and vivacity.

The Lowlanders of Scotland primarily spoke two languages; English and the Scots dialect known as "Lowland Scots" or "Lallans" (of the lowlands), which is most well known through the poetry and songs of Robert Burns. A variation of this dialect was also spoken in the Northern border country of England and survives there today where it's known as "Geordie and/or Tyneside." The Scots language, in any variant, is derived from Middle English and has no direct connection with Scots Gaelic, the Celtic language of the Highlands.—It is this lowland dialect that was carried to the Ulster Plantation by the migrants from Scotland.

During one-hundred plus years in Northern Ireland the Lallans dialect was influenced by a number of cultural factors and over time developed into a new dialect known as "Ulster Scots" or "Ullans." In its turn, Ullans was the language the Scots-Irish carried with them to America and spread throughout the frontier.

The importance of this linguistic history to our subject of the Rebel Yell has to do with aspects of the Scots language that lend themselves to a certain sound which is even more evident when a native Scots speaker uses English. This sound can best be described as a burr, trill or roll of the tongue.—As we shall see later, this same sound, done at a maniacal volume, speed and repetition, is often described as being part of some versions of the Yell.

While a few of the new emigrants settled in places such as New Hampshire and Nova Scotia, the vast majority entered America via the Delaware River and the colony of Pennsylvania. Wherever they migrated on the Eastern Seaboard the Scots-Irish were ill thought of and ill treated by the English colonists, so it didn't take long for them to follow their natural instinct and literally "head for the hills" and the frontier life they had known in Ireland.

Their first stop on the new frontier was in Western Pennsylvania where some early German emigrants had already settled. Almost immediately they squatted on Indian land and began having trouble with the colonial government and the Indians. As their numbers increased they began radiating out to the west and south, across the Alleghenies and into the Appalachians, ready to fulfill their "Hillbilly destiny."

The Scots-Irish spread rapidly into Virginia (including what is today West Virginia), North and South Carolina, Georgia and eventually Kentucky, Tennessee. Missouri and Arkansas. Some of the later emigrants arrived directly at ports in the Carolinas and also spread to the Western frontier, as well as into the Deep South.

Ultimately they found their place in the colonial hierarchy; they became the buffer between coastal "planter society" and the growing menace of the French and Indians in the Ohio Valley and elsewhere on the frontier. The colonists found "the Irish trash" useful for this less-than-desirable purpose, and so did little to harass them other than to mock their unusual ways and quaint tongue.— Out of this, another derogatory name was applied to the Calvinist Scots-Irish; they were called "Cohees" by the English from their frequent use of the term "quo'he" (quoth he).—In 1736 a Virginia landholder, William Byrd, said, "Scots-Irish from Pennsylvania, who flock over thither in such numbers, that there is not elbow room for them. They swarm like the Goths and Vandals of old and will over-spread our Continent soon. Those already settled on the River (Shenandoah) might do to stop a French musket ball!"—During the French and Indian War the Scots-Irish settlers along the frontier continued to serve this purpose, as well as some official militia duty.

By 1756 the Scots-Irish had increased in number in Western Pennsylvania to the point where they not only dominated that area but were actually able to gain control of the Pennsylvania Assembly. The original Quakers were none too pleased with their interference in politics, causing Ben Franklin to refer to them as a "mixed rabble of Scotch, Irish and foreign vagabonds, descendants of convicts [and] ungrateful rebels."

Letting none of this stop them, they continued to "swarm" further into the mountains and the frontier to the west.

When the Revolutionary War came in 1775 the Scots-Irish became stout supporters of the patriot cause. Most of them viewed it as a continuation of the fight they had been having with the British for decades, including their recent battles with the colonial government. Meanwhile, the Scots who had arrived directly from Scotland and were, for the most part, members of the coastal "planter class," remained loyal to the Crown.

In the South, the Scots-Irish concerned themselves primarily with fighting the Indian allies of the British in, and across, the Blue Ridge Mountains. They did an excellent job of removing this threat, which worked out quite well for them, as many of the soldiers intended to settle there later. Indeed, after the war the new state government gave large land grants to veterans, and former Ulstermen continued to fill the mountains and push the Indians and the frontier still further west.—In these skirmishes, it is quite possible that the battle cry which would become the Rebel Yell, was heard on American soil for the first time.

Many of the Scots-Irish in the Ohio Valley and Virginia were pressed into service in Northern theaters of the war, where their frontier abilities proved valuable in battles such as the Saratoga campaign against Burgoyne's army. George Washington even went so far as to say that if the cause was lost everywhere else he would take a last stand among the Scots-Irish of his native Virginia!

Finally, an indication of Scots-Irish numbers and impact on the war can be found in the writings of a Hessian Captain serving with the British. He wrote, "Call it not an American rebellion; it is nothing more than an Irish-Scotch Presbyterian rebellion."

Following the Revolutionary War, the new United States government had many problems to solve, not the least of which was a huge war debt that had been amassed by the various state governments as well as the Federal Government. In order to generate revenue to pay down the debt, a number of new taxes were levied on the population and on commerce; one of these was a whiskey tax. Large distillers were taxed at a rate of six cents a gallon, while the small independent producers were charged nine cents a gallon.—Now, who do you suppose most of those small independent distillers were and where they were located?... That's right! They were the Scots-Irish, in the mountains of all the Western counties.

These rural settlers were primarily farmers already living on a cash strapped budget. Distilling their grain production into the more easily transported form of whiskey and other liquor was really the only practical and reliable method they had of marketing their crop. The new tax, of course, proved burdensome…ultimately, to the point of rebellion.

Throughout the Alleghenies and Appalachians, from Pennsylvania to Georgia, the mountain distillers, often called "Whiskey Boys" harassed the federal tax collectors and marched in protest to the seats of power in the various states. As the early 1790s progressed, so did the level of violence in these civil protests. Ultimately, the tension became strong enough that armed conflict followed. The new president, George Washington, had to assemble an army of 13,000 men to confront the insurgents and put down what is known as the Whiskey Rebellion.

Several points are easily discernable from this conflict.— We now know the beginning stanza in the "ballad" that is the "Moonshiner's" long dispute with the Federal Government and the Revenue Agents. Plus, there is another chapter, named "White Lightning," that has been added to the saga of the Hillbilly.—Of more importance to our purpose, is the fact that the Scots-Irish in the South, for the first time, displayed a willingness to take up arms in open rebellion against what they perceived as unjust federal authority. Seventy years later, this willingness to fight the government would rear its head again!

With the coming of the War of 1812, the Scots-Irish found themselves in the more familiar and comfortable position of once again fighting the British! By then, they had dramatically spread out across Kentucky and Tennessee, and were beginning to cross the Mississippi and invade Missouri and Arkansas; here they would find new homes in the Ozark Mountains.

The most memorable and significant involvement the Scots-Irish settlers had in the war was at the very end of it, when they followed one of their own into battle.—Andrew Jackson was born only two short years after his parents left County Antrim, near Carrickfergus, to come to America. He was born in a part of South Carolina known as the Waxshaws, which was a strong Ulster Scots enclave. By January, 1815 he was in charge of a makeshift army getting ready to fight the British on the Chalmette flats outside of New Orleans.

His army was comprised of a few regulars, some Indians, the pirates of Jean Lafitte and a large number of Scots-Irish backwoods riflemen. In what would become known as the Battle of New Orleans, the Americans delivered the final blow of the war. Of course, "Old Hickory" would go on to become the seventh President of the United States, and the first of more than a dozen presidents of Scots-Irish descent.

The Mexican War of 1846-48, often thought to be one of the darkest chapters in United States history, was disputed along lines similar to those of the Civil War.—On relatively flimsy charges, involving the annexation of Texas and various boundary disputes associated with it, the U.S. declared war. The expansion of the country, via "Manifest Destiny," to the Pacific was closer to the actual cause. This expansion, and the war, were both strongly backed by Southern Democrats with a view toward extending slavery to new territory. Whigs, abolitionists and Northern industrialists were opposed to the war, both on the basis of land acquisition at any cost and the slavery question.

It isn't difficult to see that the Mexican War, and the reasons for its internal divisiveness, served as a prelude to the American Civil War. This was true not only on the political level, but also on the personnel side. Many of the people involved in the Mexican War would later become major players in the Civil War. They ranged from Abraham Lincoln—at the time a Whig member of the House of Representatives, and strongly opposed to the war and its slavery component—to Jefferson Davis, and both Ulysses S. Grant and Robert E. Lee, as well as many other military officers and politicians on both sides of the conflict.

This war was fought with both regular army troops and volunteers; with a great many of the volunteer units coming from Southern slave holding states, particularly Missouri, Arkansas and Louisiana. As these states were heavily populated at this time with Scots-Irish settlers, many of the volunteers were in fact from that stock.—This is one more step taken in the direction of the role they would play in a mere dozen years.

CHAPTER 4

The Scots-Irish Influence—
The Civil War: Born Fighting

Everything we have been looking at until now has been leading toward our target period of the Civil War. We have placed the Scots-Irish in the right location, with the right background and with the right attitude to take their place in the greatest American conflict of all. Yet, things have a way of not quite being as clear cut as they seem.

The Scots-Irish who had spread out across Kentucky, Tennessee, and the Deep South, as well as across the Mississippi, did, in fact, fill the role we perceive for them quite nicely. But, things were more complicated with those who were still living deep in the Appalachian Mountains.

There had long been a conflict of interests between the mountain folk and the planters in the coastal areas. The planters were mostly of Anglo-Saxon or Scottish ancestry and they were, of course, slave holders. The Scots-Irish, for the most part, did not own slaves and didn't like the political strength that the rich planters wielded. So, when war finally came, many of the mountain dwellers, at least initially, viewed it as not being their fight, and were fairly ambivalent to the Confederate cause. (A cinematic version of this can be seen in the 1965 Jimmy Stewart movie, *Shenandoah*. The Stewart character refuses to join a war that doesn't concern him, until one of his sons is captured by the Union and his property is threatened.)—This stance raised the ire of other Southerners and led to a renewed use of the derogatory term Hillbilly by the rest of the South.

There is yet another twist to this story. The area of the South that was generally considered to have the strongest Union sympathy was in the mountains of Western Virginia; so strong, that ultimately the new state of West Virginia was carved out of it. However, the most mountainous counties of the state in what is now Eastern, Southern and Central West Virginia were all pro-secession. In fact, in May 1861 they each voted for the Ordinance of Secession. The Scots-Irish soldiers from this area made up some of the staunchest and most savage supporters of the Confederacy, and many a Rebel Yell could be heard emanating from their collective throats. Because of their fierceness in battle and loyalty to the Southern cause, they were made special targets of the Union military. Indeed, then Lt. Col. Rutherford B. Hayes wrote, these counties "...are the haunts of the worst Rebel Bushwhackers in the country."

To summarize: After years of fighting the English in their native border country of Scotland the Scots-Irish moved on to the Ulster Plantation in Northern Ireland; there the Protestant Scots battled with the "outlaw" Irish chieftains and the Irish Catholics. When they moved again to America they arrived in time to fight the English once again as supporters of the patriot cause in the American Revolution. In short, as author, James Webb, has said, they were "born fighting." By the time of the Civil War the Scots-Irish had migrated throughout the hills of the Mid-South and into the Southern United States, and for the most part cast their lot with the Confederacy.

I have drawn this extensive portrait of the Scots-Irish leading up to the Civil War, both because of their importance to the Confederate Army as fighting men, and the significant role they played in the creation of the Yell. I believe that role to be the single most important ingredient, and the starting point for additional influences, that would create the diverse recipe of the Rebel Yell!

There is a great deal yet to discuss concerning the Scots-Irish influence on the Rebel Yell during the Civil War; those remaining topics will be addressed in future chapters, devoted to specifics, as we continue our investigation of the Yell.

CHAPTER 5

The Highland Scots Influence: The War Cry of the Gael

We now come to one of the most contentious aspects of discussing the Rebel Yell and its origins. This is the role that other native Scots who didn't come to America through Ireland—especially, the Highland Scots—played in the history of the Yell.

There were a relatively few Highland Scots who did in fact come through Ireland before crossing the Atlantic. The majority though, came direct from Scotland (this was also true of some Lowland Scots) and primarily settled in the Southern coastal plain as planters. (Think here in terms of "Tara" and *Gone with the Wind*.) They were, of course, Confederate gray to the core.

There is no doubt that a more substantial number of Scots-Irish fought for the South than did Highland Scots. The number of emigrants from each background dictates that this is true. The question then becomes: Which had the greater influence on the origin and sound of the Rebel Yell?

The numbers favor the Scots-Irish; additionally, their language, warlike history and rural mountain lifestyle—including a loyalty to family and mistrust of government authority—lend support to the argument on their behalf. While this is true—with the exception of the population numbers—many of the same things could be said of the Highland Scots.

Therefore, I feel that the Highland Scots part in this story shouldn't be diminished. There is, in fact, a good deal of both factual and apocryphal evidence to support their cause in this matter.

Your "New Word for the Day" is "pibroch" (ˋpi:brok). Now,

I'm sure you're thinking, "What an odd word and what does it have to do with either the Highland Scots or the Rebel Yell?"....Well, actually, it has quite a bit to do with both.

A pibroch can be either a specific musical piece or a form of music which originated in the Scottish Highlands and is performed on the traditional Highland Bagpipe. The word itself is an Anglicized version of a Scottish Gaelic word (piobaireachd) which can mean "pipering" or "pipery," (the root word is piobair which is a piper) and has through time come to refer to the oldest most traditional form of martial bagpipe music.

Among the many forms and categories of pibroch music is one known as a "Gatherings" pibroch. It is this particular form that is the most applicable to our subject. Gatherings were composed for a specific Scottish Highland clan and were used by the chieftain of the clan to rally the troops.— With its purpose not differing all that much from the Confederate battle cry, at some uncertain point, the Rebel Yell began being referred to variously as "The Pibroch of the Confederacy" or "The Pibroch of Southern Fealty." This phrase was popularized by historian Douglas Southall Freeman (see chapter 7).—For this contribution alone, the Highland Scots have claimed their place in Yell history... but there is more.

As noted above, the similarities that the less numerous Highland Scots have to the Scots-Irish are many, especially concerning background traits that played a part in the creation of the Rebel Yell.

Their mountain home in the Highlands lent itself to the same rural communication system of hollering over long distances.—They were every bit as warlike as their Lowland cousins, and during battle they also employed a blood-curdling scream as part of the Highland charge. At times "the war cry of the Gael" has been variously described as an "...eerie and disconcerting howl" and "a high, savage whooping sound," both of which bear a strong resemblance to descriptions of the Rebel Yell you'll read about later (see chapter 8). In fact, there are records from as far back as the Roman invasion of Britain which indicate a peculiar yell used by the Celtic tribes during their conflicts with the Empire's Legions.—Additionally, there is a linguistic connection between Scottish Gaelic and the battle tactic of yelling. The Gaelic, "goir" means a shrill piercing shriek; while another Gaelic word, "gaoir" translates as a cry of alarm or derision and is used in the term, "gaoir chatha" meaning "battle cry."

A "ceilidh" is a Scottish gathering that combines socializing, dancing and eating—in other words...a party. It is traditional in nature and among the traditions is one that has a current bearing on our understanding of the Yell, since it is still going on today all over Scotland. During the dancing and music, whether supplied by a piper or a band, it is common for the males present at the gathering to begin "hooching" (the "ch" pronounced as a "k"). This is an undefined sound that can either be high-pitched or one that starts low in the belly and gradually builds to a high-pitched yell or scream. Phonetic versions of the "hooch" have been indicated as, "whoooooch!" and "hee-yoooowww!"

Once again, the closeness of these descriptions to ones I've yet to discuss of the Rebel Yell, are remarkable in nature, as you shall see. Of course, the ethnic background of hooching fits in well with the overall Celtic beginnings of the Yell.

A final word about the overall influence of the Celtic race concerns the population numbers reflected in the first U.S. census near the end of the Eighteenth Century. In the Northern states, composed primarily of those in New England, approximately three-quarters of the population were Anglo-Saxon in origin; at the same time in the South about two-thirds of the people were of Celtic origin. By the time of the Civil War the Southern states—now spread out from Virginia and Florida to Missouri and Texas—showed a population that was around seventy-five percent Celtic. (Celtic in this case meaning Scots-Irish, both Highland and Lowland native Scots, Welsh, and native Irish.) Meanwhile the North, due to the 1840s influx of Irish and Germans, who had largely remained in the industrial north, saw its Anglo-Saxon numbers drop to somewhere near sixty percent.—This ethnic division makes a clear case for the important part the Celtic people played in the war effort of the Confederacy, as well as in the formation of the Rebel Yell.

CHAPTER 6

Other Influences and Theories: Hounds, War Paint and the Georgia Bull

As I've indicated, the Scots-Irish and other Celtic influences are just the starting point for studying the Rebel Yell; there are several other factors that came to bear on its development. I feel that almost all of these have merit and can be considered fairly substantial in their contribution; however others might put them in the category of theory. We are going to look at these concepts and try to deduct the likelihood of them playing a part in the Yell's history.

Hunting and Farming

The various hunting calls of the rural South are strong candidates for either being a source of the Yell or augmenting it in some manner. A member of the 9th Virginia Cavalry, Colonel (later Doctor) J. Harvie Dew (alternately, Harvey Drew—there are multiple attributions for both versions of the name) said, "Hunting, which was enjoyed and indulged in more or less by nearly every citizen of the South, was also conducive to this characteristic development (hollering)."

While any form of hunting might have spurred some sort of holler or yell, two forms in particular lent themselves to this activity.—First, would be traditional English fox hunting, a practice conducted primarily in Virginia and other parts of the coastal plain, where English and Scottish plantation owners lived. This "sport" had various calls and cries to both the horses and the dogs, which undoubtedly became a part of the Yell. In addition, the baying of the dogs could well have been imitated later by the Southern soldier during a charge as part of the Rebel Yell.—Second, is a type of hunting that belonged almost exclusively to the Scots-Irish backwoodsmen...coon hunting. Again, this activity involved different cries of communication with the hounds, which left open the same possibilities of use later in the Yell, plus repeating the howling of the hounds.

This is reinforced by J.L. McKinstry from Blue Mountain, Mississippi, who in the early 1950s wrote the following to H. Allen Smith, who we will hear more about later:

> Hunting Fox, 'coons, 'Possums, rabbits etc. Has been all but universal in the south, and even yet is common. Formerly ALL was rural. A FEW kept a pack of dogs, but every one had one or more hounds. Once the dog or dogs were on the track, yelling to them was inevitable. I have heard and given this YELL since a mere lad. The so-called 'rebel yell' was only the hunter's yell, MERGED into the army.

Whether they were fox hounds in Virginia or coon hounds in Tennessee, the soldiers' familiarity with the hunting cries and the barking of the dogs must have become a part of their Rebel Yell.—Confederate veteran, Sidney Lanier, said his group's version of the yell was "a single long cry as from the leader of a pack of hounds" (see chapter 8).

Hog-calling is a farm activity which is sometimes given credit for being a contributor to the Yell. Pork was the primary meat source for most of the rural South and with the raising of hogs there was the need for hog-calling. The sound associated with that activity is remarkably close to some versions of the Rebel Yell.

Auctioneering is an activity closely related to farming, and which has been given credit by some as either an origin of, or influence on, the Yell. In the rural South this would be particularly applicable to tobacco auctions, but could easily apply to other crops, livestock, property, etc.—I don't put much stock in this theory myself. When put to the test, it just doesn't pass muster. To my ear the two sounds are totally dissimilar, and in fact tobacco auctions didn't become a standard practice until after the Civil War.

Another quote from Colonel Dew should suffice as a final comment on the rural lifestyle of the South as it pertains to our topic: "Hollering, screaming, yelling for one person or another, to their dogs, or at some of the cattle on the plantation, with the accompanying reverberations from hilltops, over valleys and plains, were familiar sounds throughout the farming districts of the South in the days gone by."

American Indians

The influence of Native Americans on the Rebel Yell may very well be somewhat greater than is generally credited. While there are numerous mentions of it possibly having some role, very few sources go beyond that theoretic option. I believe if one looks at the basic evidence available they will find a stronger part was played by the American Indians.

Think of the proliferation of these original Americans throughout the continent when European settlers arrived. Next, consider the amount of contact, both friendly and otherwise, that the two peoples had for an extended period of time. Then look at the influence they had on one another; the adaptations of lifestyle, customs, etc. they garnered from each other. Why should we think that this "cross-culturalization" would occur in so many areas and not in this particular one? It would only be natural that having heard many an Indian war whoop and battle cry over the decades that the settlers would be familiar enough with them to be able to imitate the sound if the occasion should arise. This would be especially true of the Scots-Irish backwoodsman who had even more prolonged and up close contact. Consider this contemporary quote on the subject:

> He was a farmer so far as was needful and practicable out of the reach of all markets, though as often as not his corn was planted and his grass mown, with the long-barrelled short-stocked ponderous small-bore rifle upon which his life so often hung, placed ready and loaded against a handy stump. What sheep he could protect from the bears and wolves, together with a patch of flax, provided his family with covering and clothing. Swarthy as an Indian and almost as sinewy, with hair falling to his shoulders from beneath a coon-skin cap, a buck-skin hunting shirt tied at his waist,

his nether man was encased in an Indian breach-clout, and
his feet clad in deer-skin and moccasins.

Almost every unit in the Civil War, both North and South,
had some sort of nickname it was known by to others. The
stories behind the various names are an interesting subject
in and of themselves. But for now, we only need to be aware
of the many Southern units whose "nom de guerre" had a
Native American component. In most cases this was simply
a tribal name, such as, "Cherokee," "Seminole," "Osage,"
"Shawnee," or "Comanche" applied to a particular battalion
or regiment. The question is: Why did they have these names?
The answer ranges from, the ethnicity of the unit's personnel
and their region of origin, to the sound of their version of the
Rebel Yell. How well a given unit performed the Yell was often
a point of honor, sometimes resulting in the acquiring of their
name. In some instances, other soldiers, friend or foe, may
have bestowed the sobriquet, for example, because, "They
sound like a bunch of wild Comanches." In other cases, a
unit proudly self-named "the Cherokees" may have sounded
like Cherokee warriors because they knew from personal
experience exactly what a Cherokee war cry sounded like,
or because they were, in fact, actually Cherokee.—And that
brings us to the final point of consideration for the influence
of the Native Americans.

Soldiers with either full or mixed American Indian blood
fought on both sides of the Civil War, and in all theaters of
the war, but it can be confidently stated that a large number
of the Native Americans living in, and east of, Texas and
the Indian Territory, sided with the Confederate cause. For
those who joined the C.S.A., no matter what tribe they came
from or wherever they fought, their direct contribution to
the history of the Yell is without doubt.

It is certain that no region felt the American Indian
influence more than the Trans-Mississippi. In the Indian
Territory, that is now Oklahoma, among many other tribes,
resided what was known as the "Five Civilized Tribes." They
consisted of the Cherokee, Creek, Seminole, Choctaw and
Chickasaw Nations. Each nation was self-governing, within

the limits of their treaties with the Federal Government. These tribes had all originally been from the Southeastern United States; they had, of course, been pushed west, out of their homeland, by the U.S. Government through both war and treaty. Eventually, after treks on various routes of the "Trail of Tears" they wound up in the Indian Territory.

There were several reasons why these tribes were called civilized. They had written languages and newspapers, but had become comfortable with speaking English. Their form of government was very similar to that of the United States; while many of them farmed or ranched, they also congregated in permanent towns. To explain the final reason and its effect on the Indian Nations during the Civil War, allow me to quote from my previous book, *Creek Country*:

> Although it seems odd now...make that contradictory... there's another reason why the five tribes were considered civilized...they held slaves! In fact, the five tribes had a long history of slave culture. Consequently, they were the most effected of all the Indian tribes, both during and after...the Civil War.
>
> Because of their slave holding background, each of the five nations signed treaties with the Confederacy. In total, they sent about 6500 fighting men to the South; this included many officers as well as enlisted. There were many who fought for the Federals from the start, and others who later changed sides to the North; but they were in the minority.— There also were a number of battles and skirmishes in (and around) the territory during the conflict, particularly in border areas.—All of this had the same result in Indian Territory as it did in the rest of the nation...a weary and still divided people.

While the Choctaw and Chickasaw Nations were solidly in the Southern camp, the other three nations, in spite of the treaties they signed, were more divided; which led to a considerable amount of both intra-tribal and inter-tribal warfare. Regardless of differences within tribes—which already had a long and checkered history—there is no doubt that the greatest Indian commander of the Civil War was the Cherokee leader, General Stand Watie. He had a loyal following and more success in battle than anyone else in Indian Territory; and ultimately, at the War's end, held out longer, before surrender, than any Confederate General, Indian or otherwise.

A substantial number of the Indian enlistees performed their duties in or near the Indian Nations in the approximately thirty-one battles and skirmishes that occurred there, beginning with Wilson's Creek near Springfield, Missouri in August, 1861, through Pea Ridge, Arkansas in 1862 and concluding with Snake Creek in the Choctaw Nation in April, 1865.—At Wilson's Creek the number of Indian Territory soldiers was minimal, but it has been noted that "their chief contribution seems to have been the rousing war whoop which they had taught to their paleface comrades." The Battle of Pea Ridge was the largest engagement involving a major number of Native Americans. A soldier from the First Missouri Brigade had the following reaction when he first saw his Indian allies:

> They came trotting by our camp on their little Indian ponies, yelling forth their wild whoop...Their faces were painted, and their long straight hair, tied in a queue, hung down behind. Their dress was mostly in the Indian costume—buckskin hunting-shirts, dyed of almost any color, leggings, and moccasins of the same material, with little bells, rattles, ear-rings, and similar paraphernalia. Many of them were bareheaded and about half carried only bows and arrows, tomahawks, or war-clubs...They were... straight, active, and sinewy in their mass and movements— fine looking specimens of the red man.

Some of the soldiers from the Indian Nations did see service elsewhere; detachments went south, deeper into Texas, while others headed further east in Arkansas and beyond. At the same time, various detachments of non-Indian troops came into the territory to supplement the Indian forces.—It seems inconceivable that with this much cross contact that variations of the Rebel Yell weren't shared and adopted in both directions.—However, even if no one but the 6500 Indian Rebels ever used an Indian war cry as the Yell, then that still represents a considerable contribution to the cause.

As an interesting sidelight, there is ample evidence to suggest that Indian soldiers on both sides in the war were known to wear traditional war paint when going into battle. Although this was irregular in occurrence with both Federal and Confederate troops, the Creek warriors in Indian Territory seem to be the most well known for doing so. Again, it is hard to imagine a Native American charging into a fight, wearing war paint, and not be screaming his traditional war cry.

In his excellent book, *Civil War in the Indian Territory*, author Steve Cottrell has an interesting description of an Indian Confederate unit attacking during the First Battle of Newtonia in Southwest Missouri, in 1862: "...when Cooper's Choctaw and Chickasaw warriors, under Lt. Col. Tandy Walker, dramatically galloped right through the town in a howling charge, the blue line broke to pieces."

One of the more interesting descriptions of an Indian Nations war whoop/Rebel Yell actually comes from several decades later in the late Nineteenth Century. This is reported about the Indian outlaw, "Cherokee Bill" during an attempted jailbreak in Ft. Smith, Arkansas. Once again I quote from my book, *Creek Country*:

> Each time he fired a shot Cherokee Bill would loudly gobble like a turkey. The "gobbling" sound was an odd mixture of several noises; most seemed to think it was like the howl of a coyote combined with the gobble of a turkey. At any rate, it was a blood chilling scream that in the Indian world "signified death to anyone who heard it."—Back in the Civil War, when many Territory Indians fought for the Confederacy, they apparently used this gobble as their version of the "Rebel Yell."

Regional, State, Unit and Individual Variations

With the above information we can certainly see a pattern beginning to emerge; a pattern that indicates multiple sources of origin and/or influence for the Yell. To the Scots-Irish and Highland Scots starting point we have added various influences from farming and hunting, and the American Indian influence. Now we need to briefly consider the likelihood that even with all these influences, there is still room for additional variation.

If we were to assume that the exact same set of Yell background and influences had occurred several different times, only not in the same locale, would we expect to get several different versions of the Yell? I believe it's safe to think that an identical or a similar background from different regions or states of the South would produce something unique from each area.

Furthermore, we know that Civil War units were based on local recruiting and that most of the volunteers in any given unit came from the same town or county. Given the pride that Confederate units had in their ability to perform the Yell, this would seem to further the concept of a local flavor for the Rebel Yell.

It is equally certain that in addition to the possible variations indicated above, there had to be personal versions of the Yell which varied from individual to individual. Perhaps a Scots-Irish coon-hunter or a Native American rancher might have combined several factors and come up with something that was totally unique.

James Ervin Spivey, a soldier with the 26th Georgia was well known for his own peculiar version of the Rebel Yell. "It was a kind of scream or low, like a terrible bull, with a kind of neigh mixed along with it, and it was nearly as loud as a steam whistle." Spivey was equally famous in the Army of Northern Virginia, where he was known as the "Georgia Bull," and with the Army of the Potomac who called him "Gordon's Bull."

What we are now leaning toward is not only multiple factors in the creation of the Yell, but multiple versions of it...indeed, possibly many, many versions!

PART II: SOUND OF THE YELL

CHAPTER 7

Naming and Describing the Yell:
The Ugliest Sound and the Sweetest Music

Other than the various names for it—which we'll discuss shortly—there are three categories into which the diverse descriptions of the Rebel Yell fall:

First, is the simple word description, wherein someone tries to explain the sound of it by applying the most appropriate adjectives they can come up with, or by comparing it to some other noise or sound which may be more familiar to whomever they're explaining it to.

Second, is an attempt to spell out the sound of the Rebel Yell phonetically so that the presumed "student" can make an effort to imitate, or at least approximate, the nature of the Yell.

Third, is a specialized variation of the second category, which involves not only a phonetic description but accompanying instructions on how to best make use of the supplied phonetics.

Beginning here, and in the next two chapters, we'll be going through each of these categories in depth, using as many examples as are available for each and discussing the example's specific origin (if known) as well as the likelihood for the accuracy and veracity of each one.—Due to the multiplicity of application for some descriptions and categories, there will be occasional overlaps in their reference in these, as well as, other chapters.

So, first let's talk about...the name.

There are a number of different names—both informal and considerably more formal—which the Rebel Yell has gone by through the years.

Of course, the list begins with the common terms, the "Rebel Yell" and the shortened version, the "Yell." To the best of my knowledge, and after considerable research, it remains unknown as to the exact origin of the use of the name, the "Rebel Yell"; this is in reference equally to person, place and date. It appears that the precise information—if it ever existed—has been lost in the fog of time and the black powder smoke of the Civil War battlefield.

Another variation of the "Yell" moniker would be its use in conjunction with a specific state or unit. While I'm sure there were many references of this type in use verbally at the time, very few have come down to us in written form. One such report does exist from a soldier in Bowen's Division, First Brigade, Missouri Volunteer Infantry. On the fighting at the Battle of Champion Hill, Mississippi on May 16, 1863, Sergeant William Ruyle wrote: "They soon gave way in wild disorder. We gave the 'Missouri Yell' and took after them."

Both, the "Confederate Battle Cry" and its sister phrase, the "Southern Battle Cry" are of a slightly more formal nature, but are also shrouded in mystery as to their genesis. The general belief is that they may well have originated at the hands of the sensationalist newspapers of the time, both North and South.

Probably the most formal title is courtesy of Douglas Southall Freeman, the author of a Robert E. Lee biography and of *Lee's Lieutenants*, who referred to it as the "Pibroch of Southern Fealty." Whether or not Freeman is the originator of the phrase is uncertain. This term has been recast by others into the "Pibroch of the Confederacy." The meaning and historical connotations of these phrases have been previously discussed in reference to the Highland Scots (see chapter 5), so we will not belabor it again here.

The most informal names assigned to the Yell have undoubtedly come via anonymous Yankee soldiers of the day. While there are literally scores of variations on the theme, some of the more common and colorful include, "a damnable racket," "that blasted noise" and "a God-awful screeching." I'm certain that many more "unprintable" monikers were also given voice during the heat of battle.

The following two vignettes are difficult to classify. They

include descriptions of the Yell, but in each case it is more of a "reaction description" rather than one that actually describes the sound. The primary phrase in each could even be considered a form of name or title. At any rate, they are offered here:

A more eloquent Yankee appellation, compared to those above, was supplied by the writer, Ambrose Bierce, who, at the time, was a Lieutenant in the Army of the Cumberland, at the Battle of Chickamauga. It appears near the end of this narrative:

> At last it grew too dark to fight. Then away to our left and rear some of Bragg's people set up 'the rebel yell.' It was taken up successively and passed around to our front, along our right and in behind us again, until it seemed almost to have got to the point whence it started. It was the ugliest sound that any mortal ever heard—even a mortal exhausted and unnerved by two days of hard fighting, without sleep, without rest, without food and without hope.

The antithesis of Bierce's title, and the most personal and endearing term, came from none other than Stonewall Jackson during the Valley Campaign, who said, after listening to the Yell go around the camp one night, "That was the sweetest music I ever heard!"—Bear in mind, this came from a man, who by most accounts, had a "tin ear" of monumental proportions.—Even if Jackson had trouble accurately describing whatever it was he heard, it hasn't kept others from trying, at length, to do so....Now we'll take a look at what they've managed to come up with.

CHAPTER 8

Word and Phrase Descriptions: Catamounts, Screech Owls and Banshees

An oft repeated story says in the early part of the War, when Stonewall Jackson was very successfully on the move, that whenever soldiers heard the Rebel Yell coming from some distance away they would joke that it's either "Jackson, or a rabbit"; the implication being that the Yell sounded like the "scream or squeal of a rabbit," or, alternatively, the sound Southern hunters made when flushing a rabbit...take your pick. This is only a jumping-off-point for many other descriptions, from both the very general to the quite detailed.

Beasts of the Farm, Field and Forrest

One thing the "rabbit" description has in common with quite a few others is its reference to an animal sound. So, we'll try now to cover the specifics and backgrounds of some of those beastly noises.

There are several references to feline versions of the Rebel Yell. One, from an unknown source, describes it as the "scream of a catamount." For the uninitiated, catamount is another name for a mountain lion or panther. In the same vein, a similar comparison has been made to the screech of a wildcat or bobcat. A hunter from Florida provided a sure-fire method of hearing the yell. "All you got to do is go to the deepest and wildest part of the Everglades. Kill yourself a deer. Start draggin' the deer out of the jungle. Pretty soon a panther will get the scent. At that moment you will hear the real-for-sure rebel yell."—The author, James Street, referred to it as "something like a tomcat at midnight and the moon full" (see chapter 9).—In his bestselling book, *Confederates in the Attic*, Pulitzer Prize-winning writer, Tony Horwitz, describes one of the Yell efforts of reenactor, Robert Hodge, as "a blood-curdling, full-throated caterwaul."

These three descriptions seem to be in fairly close alignment with one another; and if anyone has heard any, or all, of the above, they may have a good idea of what some versions of the Yell sounded like. At the very least, they would have a good idea of why it was so nerve-wracking and frightening.

Now we'll move on to what can generally be grouped as canine related descriptions of the Rebel Yell. We start this roll-call with an unknown source referring to the Rebel Yell he heard as, "A peculiar shout with a close relation to a coyote yipping."—In his classic book, *The Blue and the Gray*, historian Henry Steele Commager, while acknowledging that there is little agreement on the Yell's origin or how it sounded, offers the following as one description: "It has been...described as 'a mingling of Indian whoop and wolf-howl'; it was probably born on the hunting field." This version has the advantage of being a nice combination of several theories. In addition to the animal sound (in this case, the wolf), we also get the Native American influence as well as the hunting background, which, in turn, leads us to the canine/hunting descriptions.

While apropos in various regions of the Eastern states, but particularly in Virginia, the unique calls and cries used by riders engaged in fox-hunting has given us several descriptions.—Confederate veteran and poet, Sidney Lanier, in an expanded version of his description noted earlier (see chapter 6), said his unit's Rebel Yell was "a single long cry as from the leader of a pack of hounds...a dry harsh quality that conveys an uncompromising hostility...a howl, a hoarse battle cry, a cheer, and a congratulation, all in one."—Another of Robert Hodge's versions was described by Tony Horwitz as "a quick succession of high-pitched yelps, like a foxhunter's call."

Civil War historian, Shelby Foote, relates in Ken Burns'

documentary, *The Civil War*, how an old Confederate veteran was speaking at a ladies' society meeting when he was asked to demonstrate the Rebel Yell. He declined on the basis that, "The Yell could not be done at anything less than a full run" and couldn't be done anyway with "a mouth full of false teeth and a belly full of food." However, he went on to describe the Yell as "a cross between a foxhunt 'yip' and a squalling Banshee." I think the little Celtic twist with the Banshee at the end is a nice touch; like many of the descriptions, it seems to bring together aspects of the various possible origins for the Yell.

There is mention of a few domestic farm animals; two of them more so for the humans' call to the animals rather than the animals' own sound. These would be various calls to cattle and pigs. The hog-call seems the most likely one to translate to a possible version of the Rebel Yell.—Also from the farm, we have a comparison to "the snort of a bull mixed with the neigh of a horse," courtesy of the Georgia Bull (see chapter 6).—And finally, there is an unattributed, "the screeching of nanny goats."

We still have a few more members to add to our menagerie of animal sounds.—J.M. Hill in *Celtic Warfare 1595-1763* writes of the Highlander's "...disconcerting howl" (a generic beastly sound). Tony Horwitz describes a third Robert Hodge version of the Yell as, "A peculiar, apelike grunt that rose gradually into a piercing howl." So, now we have a simian that both grunts and howls in the mix.—To this a poet has added the phrase, "starved hyena, and angry beasts."— Frank X. Tolbert, upon hearing an old veteran give the Yell, assigned it three animal comparisons. He said it sounded like "an angry elephant's scream," and later compared it to "a mountain lion and a coyote...crying in chorus." (The full story from Tolbert will come later. See chapter 12.)—Finally, we have a couple of avian related descriptions. There is one source who describes the Yell as, "Not so different from a screech owl." While another seems to think the Yell bears a resemblance to the call of the male white-winged dove.

I have the distinct feeling that we could list a number of other animal sounds that the Rebel Yell might "not be so different from" or that it "bears a resemblance to."

The Whoop Parade

The next group of attempts to describe the Yell we'll call "the whoop parade," as they all entail the use of that word. Most of these are in conjunction with the American Indian aspect of the Yell.

We have already covered the Commager description of "a mingling of Indian whoop and wolf-howl" in the preceding animal sounds section.—William Howard Russell, a war correspondent for *The Times* (New York) and later the author of *My Diary North and South*, offered a description of the Rebel Yell which included a jab at the Confederates: "the Southern soldiers cannot cheer, and what passes muster for that jubilant sound is a shrill ringing scream with a touch of the Indian war-whoop in it." While I don't believe it was a matter of "cannot cheer," it is indeed true that in comparison to the Union soldiers, the Confederates "did not cheer." This has been referenced above and will be dealt with at greater length later.—There is also the generic, and un-attributable, description: "similar to an Indian war whoop."—Of course, all of these descriptions lead me back to the conclusion that the Native American influence can be heard in the Yell, both directly from those groups siding with the South, and indirectly from the non-Indian Confederates who learned or imitated what they heard.

Going back to the Scots influence, we find in MacLeod's *Highlanders—A History of the Gaels* the following: "The terror was heightened by...the distinctive war-cry of the Gael—a high, savage whooping sound...." Coupled with Hill's "disconcerting howl" from the previous section, I view this as further reinforcement for the concept of Celtic influence on the Yell.

Finally, our whoop parade concludes with a mention of the fact that at Texas A&M University the Corp of Cadets has a "whoop yell" that is supposedly derived from the Rebel Yell.

The chief argument for this belief is that Confederate General Lawrence Sullivan "Sul" Ross served as the University's President during the 1890s when the whoop yell was started and should have had considerable knowledge of the Rebel Yell (or, at least, the Texas version of it). Plus, the students of that era would have had many living family members and friends who were veterans of the War and familiar with the Yell. When you add in the fact that Sul Ross, who also served as a Texas Ranger and the Governor of Texas, among other functions, was a prominent Indian fighter, both before and after the Civil War, leaving him with direct knowledge of the Indian war whoops of the Comanches, Wichitas, Kickapoos and other tribes, there is a somewhat surprising credibility to the Texas A&M story, which also brings us full-cycle back to the Native American influence.—It should be mentioned that several other colleges have their version of the Rebel Yell as part of their tradition. They include the Virginia Military Institute, the University of Mississippi and the University of Nevada-Las Vegas.

Screams and Shrieks

The next group we'll call the "hear no evil" category in honor of the little monkey who covered his ears and the Yankee soldiers who did the same. The overall description which applies to this group, as well as a number of others, is simple enough: the Rebel Yell was both prolonged and high-pitched, to the point of having a squeal or forced falsetto quality about it, also described as "...a long, quavering sound..."

First, there are two descriptions which seem to pertain particularly to the Scottish influenced Yells: One is simply a reference to a "high-pitched scream." The other is a slightly more elaborate version describing a "shriek with a shrill piercing voice."—Next is one that is comparable to Robert Hodge's "apelike grunt" version. A reporter for the New Orleans *Times Picayune* wrote, "It paragons description, that yell! How it starts deep and ends high, how it rises into three increasing crescendos and breaks with a command of battle" (see chapter 11).—Another unknown

source has described it as a "strange, eerie scream."—
Confederate Colonel Kellar Anderson has provided us
with the following: "that penetrating, rasping, shrieking,
blood-curdling noise." In the next section we will hear
about another of Colonel Anderson's descriptions of the
Yell.—One particularly well known yeller (the Georgia
Bull again) was so loud and shrill he was said to sound like
a steam whistle.

The financier and statesman, Bernard Baruch, who was
born in South Carolina and whose father, Dr. Simon Baruch
was a surgeon on Robert E. Lee's staff during the War,
recalls a wonderful memory in his autobiography, *My Own
Story*. He relates how whenever the song *Dixie* was played
or sung his father would jump to his feet and start letting
go with the Rebel Yell, no matter the circumstances at the
time: "As soon as the tune started Mother knew what was
coming and so did we boys. Mother would catch him by the
coattails and plead, 'Shush, Doctor, shush.' But it never did
any good. I have seen Father, ordinarily a model of reserve
and dignity, leap up in the Metropolitan Opera House and
let loose that piercing yell."

In the same vein as the presiding story there is a vignette
from Clyde Brion Davis' book *"The Great American
Novel~~"* in which the lead character, Homer Zigler,
describes what he saw and heard while attending a showing
of D.W. Griffith's film *The Birth of a Nation*. He was sitting
in the balcony watching a particularly thrilling action scene
when "…an old man downstairs leaped up in his seat, waved
his hat and let out a blood-curdling yell. No doubt he was
a Southerner himself and probably had taken part in just
such an event in his youth."

And thus, we have two more "cover your ears" moments.

Others

The following section is comprised of various descriptions
which defy inclusion in any of the other categories.

First, is an account written by a Confederate soldier
following the Battle of the Wilderness who manages to draw

three different and distinct comparisons for the sound of the Yell:

> At first [the Rebel Yell] heard like the rumbling of a distant train, it came rushing down the lines like the surging waves upon the ocean, increasing in loudness and grandeur, and passing, it could be heard dying on the left in the distance. Again it was heard coming from the right to die away again on the distant left. It was renewed three times, each with renewed vigor. It was a yell like the defiant tones of a thunderstorm.

Don Bracken, Senior Editor of History Publishing and a Civil War writer, has beautifully described the Yell as, "an audible sensation of being overwhelmed." (In chapter 11, concerning sound recordings, we will cover his story in more depth.)

The First Battle of Bull Run (Manassas) is one of the most well known of the War. Out of that encounter we have acquired two additional descriptions: The first involves Stonewall Jackson again. During a bayonet charge on Henry House Hill, General Jackson gave his troops the order to "yell like furies."—A Federal soldier is said to have credited General Beauregard's forces at First Manassas with emitting an "unearthly wail" during their charge. (See chapter 13.)

Echoing the Union soldier at Manassas, there is N.B. Hogan of the 11th Alabama writing about Gaine's Mill: "At length the furious Rebel yell was heard....With a 'wild, unearthly yell' the whole line sprang forward, and...were upon...the enemy, who, without much resistance...gave up the fight...."

In addition to the previous description attributed to him, Colonel Kellar Anderson of Kentucky's Orphan Brigade, also alliteratively referred to the Yell as, "that maniacal maelstrom of sound." (In chapter 14 we will discuss Colonel Anderson and relate the entire story from which these two descriptions were derived.)

Then we have historian Henry Steele Commager providing us with yet another description. This time we find that the Rebel Yell was "more overpowering than the cannon's roar." Actually, Commager's "overpowering" and Bracken's "overwhelmed" seem to be a nice fit with one another.

Another description by Union soldiers is "a sort of swirling, discordant scream that grew louder and more horrible as the attackers approached."

A clean, compact and accurate assessment of the Yell by a Web history writer is that, "It is the sound of desperation."

Finally, we're back to the category I call "reaction descriptions," which I touched on earlier in chapter 7 concerning names. They don't attempt to describe the Yell itself, but rather are about tangential responses.

The following two reactions are reportedly from Union soldiers after hearing it for the first time: One Yank talked about "a peculiar corkscrew sensation that went up your spine when you heard it." Another said, "There is nothing like it on this side of the infernal region." Neither of these gives us any idea what the Rebel Yell sounded like, but they certainly give us an idea of the effect it had on the enemy.

As usual, the late historian, Shelby Foote, may have given us the most concise and accurate response: "If you claim you heard it and weren't scared that means you never heard it!"

CHAPTER 9

Phonetic Descriptions:
Keeooks, Yips and Who-eys

First of all, it needs to be stated that phonetics is a large and complex scientific field of study which has many different branches. To clarify, we are dealing with "simple phonetics," the attempt to spell out a sound using the standard alphabet. Other branches of phonetics are far too complicated to be addressed here.

One of the primary goals of Yell enthusiasts is an accurate, readable, repeatable, phonetic version of the Rebel Yell. This, of course, has proven to be just as elusive as other descriptions have been. On the surface this would seem a difficult, if not impossible, task, especially given the substantial number of Yell variations that appear to exist. Plus, there would naturally be differences of opinion as to how to convert the sounds to phonetic spelling, as well as the interpretation that different people would have of the phonetics. However, none of the above has kept people, over the last 140 plus years, from repeatedly trying to accomplish this feat, as we shall see below.

Without doubt, certain phonetic versions of the Yell have more authenticity than others, but in an effort to be inclusive we will cover all that are available. Many of these, but certainly not all, have been gleaned from author H. Allen Smith's book *The Rebel Yell*, a 1950s humorous satire on the South. Its tone can be best understood by the book's sub-title: *Being a Carpetbagger's Attempt to Establish the Truth Concerning the Screech of the Confederate Soldier Plus Lesser Matters Appertaining to the Peculiar Habits of the South*. As attorney and historian, Monte Akers, has pointed out, the book did not survive the decade with its ability to "invoke mirth" fully intact. Nonetheless, it does contain a substantial number of phonetic versions of the Yell, most of them from individuals in the South with varying degrees of credentials pertaining to the topic, but none of them from Civil War veterans.

Among the versions which I'm afraid have little to back them are the following: A 1952 *Time* magazine article attempting to describe what amounts to a modern take on the Rebel Yell. This unlikely entry appeared in print as "Eee-Yow!" As H. Allen Smith indicated in his book, this version is much too generic and has been heard in many other situations, including from a man who has just been kicked in the groin during a bar fight....It can't possibly be right!—Another generic version is the classic "Yee-haw!" This one has been a favorite of the movies and television for many years, but once again its use for other purposes fails to give it the uniqueness that is normally attributed to the Rebel Yell.—Speaking of movies, we have to acknowledge the 1939 classic film *Gone with the Wind* and its version of the Yell. While it fulfills the requirements of being both repetitively prolonged and high-pitched, one has to question the basic nature of this version, which went: "Yay-hoo! Yay-hoo! Yay-hoo!" Once again we are faced with the same problem that plagued the previous two entries; it is simply too general in both nature and application.

An animal related spelling of the Yell (related specifically to a panther) was supplied to Smith as follows: With the tongue stuck firmly in the side of the mouth and without removing it, yell "Keeook!" It turns out this version comes from some Northern Boy Scouts of the Panther Patrol who use this cry on their outings....So much for authenticity!

The next four versions all appear to be at least somewhat questionable, even though they have avoided the troubles afflicting those listed above. Their various problems range from the lack of credentials, to inconsistency, to overblown pomposity for each source. The only thing the versions have in common is that they come from mid-1950s Southerners of varying occupations. The four are the result of an argument over the nature of the Rebel Yell at a party in

Chapel Hill, North Carolina which H. Allen Smith attended.

The first, came from noted Civil War historian, James Street, who said he absolutely knew how it went and proceeded to give out with a mighty "Rrrrrr-yahhhhhhhhhhhhh-yip-yip-yip-yip-yip!" The five "yips" at the end were uttered rapidly and in a high, piercing tone. (Another, albeit unknown, source has also given a multiple "yip-yip-yip" version.) Despite Mr. Street's credentials, a problem exists due to the fact that in a newspaper article at a later date he was quoted as follows:

> Actually, there were as many kinds of rebel yells as there were rebels. My own favorite was whooped years ago at Confederate reunions. It wound up with a scream, well oiled by bourbon and branch water—it sounded something like, "Ye-e-e-e—Ywoh-h-h!"—something like a tomcat at midnight and the moon full. I'm sure, though, that despite all the declarations to the contrary, there will be folks talking and writing about the rebel yell for years to come. I have learned that it is easier to sell myths than to kill them.

How the man could make those outrageous assumptions about the future of Rebel Yell research is beyond me!...I really don't know what he's talking about!...Do you?...Okay, okay! So he was right!

Given all the "yipping" referenced above, now would be a good time to note the credence of the concept that the Rebel Yell was based on hog calling. The theory says that a hog-call sounds something like this: "Hooooooooooooooo-eeeeeeeeeee! Hooooooooooooooo-eeeeeeeeeeeee!" followed by: "Pig, pig, pig, pig, pig!" if you're calling hogs, and followed by: "Yip, yip, yip, yip, yip!" if you're chasing Yankees.—As always, this one is left to your judgment.

Nevertheless, getting back to the cocktail party argument, a competing version came from a professor of Southern English (giving it a slight aura of veracity) and was a simple "Yeeeeee-eeeeeow!"—The next, was delivered up by a shoe merchant (head scratching is allowed at this point) who was certain that the true sound was a prolonged "Whooooooooooooooooo-wow!"—Finally, we have the offering of a policeman who came to break up the argument after it spilled out into the street. He said they were all "peckerwoods" who didn't know what they were yelling about and provided the following version: "Ffffweeeeeeeeeeee-up!"—As usual, it's best not to fight the law.

Meanwhile, in Charleston, South Carolina, a prominent attorney, thought by his peers to be an expert on the Civil War and the Rebel Yell, (a definite degree of qualification, no doubt) gave his version to H. Allen Smith as follows: "Yuhhhhh-wooooooooo-eeeeeee-UH!" He was long, loud and confident, according to Smith. However, with apologies to all attorneys of my acquaintance, it should be remembered that those three traits are already built into the genes of most lawyers.

Dr. Douglas Southall Freeman was a renowned historian, Civil War authority and biographer of Robert E. Lee. When he was visited in his Richmond, Virginia home by Smith he gladly passed on his version of the Yell, with special instructions as to its proper use. His Rebel Yell was as follows: "Yeeeeeeeeeee-ahhhhhhhhhhh!" He indicated that the "Yeeeeeeeeeee" of the Yell began in the key of "F" and descended the scale, with sustained volume, through the "ahhhhhhhhhhh!" and ended sharply in the key of "A." On the surface, given the qualifications of Dr. Freeman and the definitive nature of his Yell (*with instructions*) it would appear that we hit the "mother lode." Unfortunately, Dr. Freeman had the same problem as James Street before him… inconsistency; later he also came up with another version. When composer, Richard Bales, was working on his cantata *The Confederacy* he wanted to include the Rebel Yell as its conclusion. To make it authentic, he went to Dr. Freeman for help. The good doctor promptly yelled the following: "Ooooooo-eeeeeeee!" Bales said, "Once having heard it, you never forget it."—Forget it…no! Be confused by it…yes!

Another doctor, with impeccable credentials as both a Southerner and historian, is Dr. Bell Irvin Wiley who is most well known for authoring both *The Life of Johnny Reb* and *The Life of Billy Yank*. He concedes that "The Confederate yell is hard to describe….on the field of combat, the Rebel yell was an unpremeditated, unrestrained and utterly informal 'hollering.' It had in it a mixture of fright, pent-up nervousness, exultation, hatred and a pinch of pure deviltry..." Ultimately, he cites various veterans who said the Rebel Yell went like this: "Yai,yai,yi,yai,yi!"—While not identical, this version plays well with one from a Northern newspaper reporter covering the Battle of Hatcher's Run. He wrote the Confederates charged "with the invariable 'yei, yei, yei' of the Rebel."—Another very similar variation has it "more like 'Yee Yee Yee Yee!'"

Dr. Wiley gives us one more version of the Yell, although it can be found in many other locations. It is the version given by the previously mentioned Colonel J. Harvie Dew (see chapter 6), of the 9th Virginia Cavalry, who is considered by many to be the most authoritative—and/or most cited—version to be put in print.

In an 1892 article in *Century Illustrated Magazine*, and a similar article nearly twenty years later in 1911 for *Confederate Veteran*, Volume 19, Colonel Dew, who served under J.E.B. Stuart, detailed the version of the Rebel Yell used by his unit during battle. The articles address a number of interesting issues, so the Colonel will be cited several more times before we are finished. But for now we need to address the core issue of how the Yell sounded, as found in both articles. First, the key passage from the *Century Illustrated Magazine* article:

> In an instant every voice with one accord vigorously shouted the "Rebel Yell," which was so often heard on the field of battle. "Woh-who-ey! who-ey! who-ey! Woh-who-ey! who-ey!" etc. (The best illustration of this "true yell" which can be given the reader is by spelling it as above, with directions to sound the first syllable "woh" short and low, and the second "who" with a very high and prolonged note deflecting upon the third syllable "ey.")

Next, we have the comparable section from the *Confederate Veteran* article:

> The "Rebel Yell" was usually preceded in reaching the very high note with the syllable "wah." Thus: "Wah, who-ey,

who—ey, who—ey." The first syllable was uttered with a low, short note, followed by the "who" uttered with a very high, prolonged tone, deflecting on the "ey." The high note was often held on a very long expiration, giving to it a protracted tone; thus, "Who—ey," and so was the "yell" kept up.

While there are differences, the two descriptions are very similar with the most notable exception being the "first syllable" spelling; "Woh" in the first and "Wah" in the second. Whether this represents a misprint, a memory lapse after twenty years or an intentional correction by Dew is anyone's guess at this advanced point in time.

Three very similar, but not identical, versions of the Yell have been provided by various Federal soldiers. An unknown Yank said of his experience at Gettysburg: "They staggered, but closed up, and with the familiar 'Hi-yi!' returned our fire and pressed forward with the savage courage of baited bulls."—Gilbert Adams Hays, among a number of other comments, wrote: "...when the Johnnies charged, it was with their never-ceasing 'ki-yi' until we found them face to face."—A surgeon with the 4th New York recalled: "Suddenly out of the dusk in front, and to the rear of us, burst the 'Ki-yi Ki-yi' close to us and with it the Rebels were seen."

Another version with some similarity to the three above is said to have its roots in the Native American war cry. It is "a high-pitched, three toned 'hi EEE ya!'"

A couple of Southern newspapers had their say about the Yell in response to H. Allen Smith, when he first printed the versions he had collected. Of course, both of them said he was wrong on all counts and offered their own renditions.—In Winston-Salem, North Carolina the *Twin City Sentinel* said the only true Rebel Yell goes like this: "Eeeeeeee-YUH-haaeeeeooooooooo!"—Meanwhile, down the road, the editors at the Asheville, North Carolina *Citizen* said the correct version of the Yell was as follows: "Y-Yo-Yo—Wo-Wo!"...and they cited no less of an authority than the *Encyclopedia Americana.*—What can we make of this journalistic dichotomy? Not much, I'm afraid, other than its reinforcement of the old saying,

"Don't believe everything you read in the newspapers."

Earlier we looked at the Yell used in the film version of *Gone with the Wind* and dismissed it as highly unlikely, but when reviewing the rendition spelled out in the novel itself, we can't be quite so dismissive. Although it was published seven decades after the Civil War, the classic book was written by a true daughter of the South, Margaret Mitchell, whom, it is assumed, had access throughout her life to many firsthand accounts of the War, including the Rebel Yell. Her version is as follows: "yee-aay-eee!" As we shall see later, some new research does nothing to discount this version and may indeed reinforce it.

The last rendition of the Yell we'll examine is the phonetic transcription of the version given by some very old veterans at the 75th Anniversary of the Battle of Gettysburg, which was captured on film. (We'll discuss this event in more detail in chapter 10.) For now, we'll focus on the phonetics. The generally accepted transcription of this version of the Rebel Yell is as follows: "Wa-woo-woohoo, wa-woo-woohoo!" I think it's safe to say that this rendition bears at least a passing resemblance to the second J. Harvie Dew version cited above.

The fact that this final version was captured on film leads us easily into the topic of our next chapter.

CHAPTER 10
Recorded Versions of the Rebel Yell—Part I:
D.W. Griffith, William Randolph Hearst and Ken Burns

The long sought after "Holy Grail" of Yell research has been to find an actual recording of the Rebel Yell performed by someone who knew exactly what it sounded like, because he was in fact a Confederate soldier who had used it in battle. Ideally, this recording would have been made in the very early days of sound recording when whatever veteran involved was not yet terribly old and still had the Yell fresh in his memory. But, alas, this treasure is yet to be found, if it even exists. However, we do have a few versions which made their way onto various recording media and have subsequently found their way to daylight. Thanks to modern electronic technology, these recordings have been saved, enhanced and made easily accessible to the public.

So, for the next three chapters, let's take a look at what recordings we actually have available to us, and how we can go about seeing and/or listening to them. Let's begin with…

Recordings on Film

Through the years the Rebel Yell has been used in countless Hollywood movies and television shows. Without doubt, the renditions heard in these productions can be described as artificial at best; after all, Hollywood is the capital of make believe. These various generic film versions, used throughout the "Golden Age" of movies and well into the middle and late twentieth-century, including the *Gone with the Wind* version, don't make the cut at any level and certainly don't meet our criteria for the "Grail."

With the increase in popularity of Civil War reenacting, which occurred in the later part of the twentieth-century, it can be accurately said that film versions of the Yell did improve. Production companies took advantage of the numerous, dedicated reenactors, using them as extras to fill the battle scenes more realistically, both in appearance and sound. But the question still remained: How close were they to the real sound, or sounds, of the Rebel Yell? Moreover, no matter what the answer might be to that question, it still is not what we are looking for on our quest.

It's ironic that two of the best chances to get the Rebel Yell on film never happened!—At the time of D.W. Griffith's epic film *The Birth of a Nation*, based on Thomas Dixon's novel *The Clansman*, which we mentioned earlier, there were still plenty of Southern veterans alive and kicking who could have helped in providing an authentic rendition of the Yell....But, alas, the year was 1915 and we were still in the silent movie era.

The next good opportunity came in 1934 when Cosmopolitan Pictures, a production company owned by William Randolph Hearst, made a Civil War movie titled *Operator 13* for MGM, starring Marion Davies—who had been Hearst's longtime mistress—Gary Cooper and Sidney Toler among others.

In the movie, Davies plays a Northern actress named Gail Loveless recruited by the Union to be a spy (code name: Operator 13). She goes to a Confederate military ball disguised as an "octoroon" maid, where she hears, and then passes on, critical information to the Federals. Later, undercover as a Southern sympathizer named Anne Claybourne, she meets Gary Cooper's character, Confederate Captain Jack Galliard, a spy for the South who has been assigned to find the Union spy and kill her. They fall in love, but eventually both realize the true identity of the other. Captain Galliard, bound by duty, arrests her anyway just as he is about to be captured by the Federals. Davies' multi-role character, bound by love, helps him to escape so they can meet again after the War.

In spite of the unlikely nature of the storyline, there was an apparent desire to be as authentic as possible when it came to battle scenes. It was nominated for an Academy

Award for cinematography and, in an effort to get the Rebel Yell correct, a very interesting sound recording was made of the Yell, which we will learn more about in chapter 11. Unfortunately, for reasons unknown, this recording never found its way onto the final sound track of the film... another opportunity lost.

The only version on film of the Rebel Yell, with valid credentials, didn't come from the fertile imagination of Hollywood writers and directors, but from the film journalists whose newsreel productions played at theaters before the feature film.

As mentioned in the previous chapter, in 1938 at Gettysburg, a 75th Anniversary Reunion of the battle was held with some of the remaining veterans from both the North and South. A newsreel film taken as the old-timers shook hands across the famous wall includes several of the Confederate Veterans giving a relatively mild attempt at the Rebel Yell. Given their voices, which had been weakened with age, it was a good-natured effort and still had some of the high-pitched quality associated with the Yell.

While this newsreel has us getting warmer in our search, there are still several problems. The first, we just alluded to: Age, weakened voices and failing memories make for a less than stirring version of the Yell, however authentic it might be. Second, is the sound on the film itself. It is, after all, a newsreel shot in the field rather than in a studio with proper sound equipment. The old veterans were at some distance from the camera and field microphone when the footage was made. Also, by today's standards, the relatively primitive nature of that recording equipment presents several quality issues.

Nevertheless, this newsreel is of considerable interest as it represents the only known, valid version of the Rebel Yell committed to film, and the first to be readily available to the public via its use in theaters.

Today, it can be viewed at a number of internet sites (some of which will be listed in Appendix A), as well as in two well-known Civil War documentaries. It appears in

Volume II of the video *Echoes of the Blue and Gray* and in the final episode of Ken Burns' *Civil War*.

There is also an "audio only" version of a simulated battle charge made from the newsreel (which will be listed in Appendix B).

It's now time to move on to the next part of our examination.

CHAPTER 11

Recorded Versions of the Rebel Yell—Part II: Duane Eddy, Arturo Toscanini and the UDC

Before going any further, a quick word about wax recordings: For those of you who are not familiar with early wax recordings, both cylinder and disc, don't let the word "wax" throw you. The material in question was a hardened wax and was similar in appearance and feel to other materials used later in the recording business, such as vinyl. The primary difference was in the greater thickness of the disc or cylinder, which was necessary to accommodate the properties of the wax and make them less susceptible to damage.—A concern about damage will come into play later.

Audio Recordings

Much like with films, there have been attempts down through the years to simulate the Rebel Yell on audio recordings. Again, as with films, the results have not been very good, primarily because they were artificial—some record producer's idea of the Yell. Without recounting them individually, suffice it to say, there have been several Rock-n-Roll and Country Western records which fit the category. (Duane Eddy's *Rebel Rouser* and Billy Idol's *Rebel Yell* are a couple of examples.)

In the earlier chapter on phonetics I mentioned another recording from a decidedly different genre: Richard Bales' semi-classical cantata *The Confederacy*, which has the chorus shouting Dr. Freeman's second version of the Rebel Yell at the end of a solid rendition of *Dixie*. In 1954 Columbia Records issued an album of the same title, which, with a little effort, can still be found in vintage record stores and on the internet.—Another semi-classical version of *Dixie* was recorded live at a 1950 concert in Richmond, Virginia. Well-known conductor, Arturo Toscanini, leading the NBC Orchestra, played *Dixie* as an encore; the enthusiastic audience tagged on their versions of the Rebel Yell to the finish of the song. If desired, this recording can also be located fairly readily as well. The real questions here are: Would you want to buy either of these recordings, and why? If you decide to purchase either, or both, my suggestion would be to buy the records for the quality music on them rather than for the Rebel Yells. (Later, I will give you an even better alternative for acquiring these recordings.)

The next recordings to be discussed are, without doubt, the most important ones we have yet encountered. As is often the case when dealing with historical research, the story of these recordings is a bit cloudy at times and hard to follow...but also, incredibly interesting. So, I'll do my best to be as accurate as possible, sort out the details of the story and try to make sense of it all.

The recording that is absolutely closest to fulfilling our requirements, if it truly exists, and can be found, verified and accurately transcribed, is a wax cylinder recording supposedly made in the late Nineteenth-Century (1898 being the most commonly cited year). Very few details are available about this recording other than it was made at a United Daughters of the Confederacy (UDC) convention which was likely held in Florida.

The obvious importance of this recording, other than its very existence, lies in the time frame involved. If it, in fact, was recorded when the various rumors about it indicate, it could have been made by a veteran who was only in his fifties. Since there is no mention of the individual who did the Yell for the recording, his age must remain uncertain; but, regardless of this missing information, the proximity of the recording to the War's end would give this purported treasure a currency that would be undeniable. There is also the possibility that the wax cylinder might contain more than one voice performing the Yell; if so, it would be of even more importance.

The residing place of this recording was, for many years, thought to be with the UDC at their national headquarters in Richmond, Virginia; unfortunately, to date, it has never surfaced, leaving us, for the time being, with only an enticing mystery.

The information concerning the above recording now gets tangled up a bit with what we know about the next possible recording. Another UDC convention was held in Jacksonville, Florida during November, 1931 at which the members passed a resolution, with the stated purpose being to "have the Rebel Yell preserved for posterity by means of a Victrola record."

As a consequence of the UDC resolution a meeting was held in New Orleans on February 19, 1932, supposedly to fulfill the resolution's purpose. A 1932 issue of the *Confederate Veteran* magazine says:

> A gala occasion…was the coming together of Confederate veterans of the city and vicinity…to test their ability to make the welkin ring again with the Rebel Yell, that indescribable cry which was wont to stir the Confederate soldier to deeds of valor….The resolution has aroused considerable interest, and inquiries have been made as to the nature of the Yell— 'and what, if any, were the words to it?' It is something that cannot be described—that must be heard.

It would appear that by 1932 there was some legitimate confusion about the Rebel Yell, even in the Deep South.

The magazine article goes on to quote from an article in the New Orleans *Times-Picayune* which covered the meeting. This same article is the one which gave us the well-known description of the Yell referred to earlier in chapter 8: "How it starts deep and ends high, how it rises into three increasing crescendos…" It can be fairly assumed that because this was a contemporary article and description it could only have been based on the Rebel Yell as the writer heard it at the New Orleans veteran gathering, that is, after all, what he was covering for his newspaper. The *Times-Picayune* article went on to read:

> The spirit...came back to those veterans of the war when they forgot their eighty or ninety years and were back on the edge of the fight.
>
> Behind the crowd the gray ranks formed once more. Histories state that New Orleans sent 20,000 fighting men to battle for the Southern Cause. When the ranks formed again Saturday, fourteen of those 20,000 were present to record the cry that inspired Louisianians in many battles.
>
> 'Attention! Forward, March!'
>
> The crowd opened up. Flags were lifted high and hats were removed, as the veterans filed proudly into the center of a circle.
>
> Singly they tried their vocal strength, to much applause, then it was—
>
> 'All right, boys! Lets all go together now.'
>
> From throats that had given the weird cry seventy years ago as Louisianians charged into battle came the same eerie notes of the yell that is referred to as 'awe-inspiring' and 'nerve racking' in annals of the war.
>
> Veterans turned and patted each other. The crowd cheered with glee. The 'Girls of the Sixties' applauded and waved Confederate flags.

According to the magazine article there were twenty-five "Women of the South" in attendance, all over eighty years of age, who cheered and sang Southern songs.

What neither the magazine nor newspaper article makes clear is if, in fact, a recording was made of the proceedings. It was the intended purpose of the meeting. The newspaper says the fourteen veterans "were present to record the cry..." But no where does it state that the recording was actually made, and more importantly, what was to become of it.

If the recording existed, it would be natural to assume that it would have found its way to the UDC headquarters in Richmond. If it still exists, the UDC, nor anyone else, seems to know where it might be.—Another mystery which someday may be unraveled.

The next recording of the Rebel Yell we're going to look

at involves a fellow named Thomas N. Alexander, a private in Co. I, 37th North Carolina Infantry Regiment. Confusion abounds concerning both this old veteran and the recording he made.

It appears that there were four different Thomas Alexanders in the 37th North Carolina, each from a different company and each with a different middle initial. With the sometimes chaotic record keeping and newspaper reporting during the War, coupled with the circumstance of four soldiers with the same name in one unit, it is little wonder that mistakes were made after the War; biographies and obituaries were jumbled where these four men were concerned.—The best available information says our man, Thomas N. Alexander of Co. I, appears to have joined in February, 1862 in Charlotte. His first action was seen in June of that year at the Battle of Gaines Mill (also known as First Cold Harbor). It was at Gaines Mill that Alexander said he first heard and used the Rebel Yell. In 1864, at Fusel's Mill, he received an unspecified wound.—It should be noted that a major resource book, *North Carolina Soldiers*, has partially conflicting information (due, at least to some degree, to the problems listed above). It shows him joining in 1864 at Liberty Mills, close to Orange, Virginia. Also, according to the book, Thomas R. Alexander received a leg wound at Gettysburg, while Thomas N. Alexander's obituary states that he was wounded in the leg in 1864 (possibly at Fusel's Mill, but also possible confusion with Thomas R.).

As I indicated, things don't get any clearer when we start tracing the history of Alexander's recording of the Yell. The only thing the various accounts agree on is that radio station WBT in Charlotte did make a recording of Alexander doing his version of the Rebel Yell. Also, it is generally agreed that at least one recording was made at a Sons of Confederate Veterans meeting. Most sources believe this occurred in 1935, although others list the year as 1929 or 1932.

In one version of the story, the radio station's general manager sat down with Alexander at the meeting to discuss the War and particularly the Yell. This interview was being recorded, and near its end the station manager asks the other old veterans attending the meeting to give the Rebel Yell along with Alexander. They make a rather weak attempt, reminiscent of the veterans in the Gettysburg film, and that ends the recording session. (This is a list of the ex-Confederates who participated in this group recording, along with their ages: T.N. Alexander, age 92; H.C. Irwin, age 90; W.B. Kidd, age 84; D.W. Mayes, age 91; and J.E. Porter, age 96.)—At a later time during the meeting, Alexander is taken by the general manager to a more secluded room and asked to record his version of the Yell solo…and a wonderful job he does!

A variation of the story about the second recording, has it being made sometime after the meeting, only now it takes place at the WBT studio in Charlotte, instead of in a meeting room.—Whichever ending you choose to believe, this basic story is the one that goes with 1935 as the year the recording was made. One problem does exist, however: Alexander's age could not have been 92 in 1935! It is known that he was active in Confederate veteran groups until his death in 1940 at the age of 95, making him 90 in 1935.

Another version of the story says the group recording at the meeting, as well as Alexander's solo recording in the studio, were both made several years earlier; supposedly, as mentioned above, one in 1929 and the other in 1932. Which one occurred in which year is not entirely clear, but once again, Alexander's listed age of 92 at the time of the group recording doesn't fit with either of these years.

The main thing to take away from this is that we finally have, in spite of Thomas N. Alexander's age, a robust, well-recorded, authentic version of the Rebel Yell with a great deal of provenance. Thanks to Alexander's grandson, J.B. Joye of Belmont, North Carolina, this recording was not only saved, but was made available to the public through the website of the 26th North Carolina Regiment reenactment unit. It has since appeared on several other sites as well. (The website for the 26th N.C. and some of the others will be listed in Appendix A.)…And still this recording's story is not finished!

In late 2004 and early 2005, after the recording had been

on the internet for a while, and had started to make the rounds among reenactors, Don Bracken, Senior Editor of the History Publishing Company, whom I quoted earlier, decided to examine it more closely. History Publishing used modern sound technology to clarify the old recording and to take it a step further; using multiple tracts of the original recording, each one varied by volume and pitch, they simulated the sound of a company of Confederate soldiers (about 70 to 100 men) in full charge against a Federal line. (See Appendix A for website.) Don Bracken's full quote on the results of the new recording is as follows: "The effect was startling. It wasn't a frightening sound in the nightmarish or fiendish sense. It was an audible sensation of being overwhelmed. It was like having a sonic tidal wave approach you. What might have unnerved the Union soldiers who reportedly fled from it was a sense of helplessness."...Now we're getting somewhere!

In the previous chapter on film recordings, we discussed the Civil War drama, *Operator13*, and the Yell recording that was made for it, but which was never used in the movie. Now it's time to look closer at the rest of the story concerning that particular recording.

When Cosmopolitan Pictures and MGM started looking around for someone to record an authentic Yell for them, they found a veteran, Sampson Saunders Simmons, conveniently living nearby in Los Angeles. During the War he had been a courier in Co. E of Stuart's 8th Virginia Cavalry, and, at the time, was serving as Commander of the Pacific Division of the United Confederate Veterans.

On April 10, 1934 Simmons went to the studio and made the recording of his version of the Yell. Again, as with Alexander, I can attest to the fact that the old veteran did a fine piece of work that day. As I indicated earlier, in spite of all this effort and preparation, within a short period of time the decision was made not to use the recording in the film. So, a mere seventeen days after being recorded, the wax disc was presented by MGM, in a small ceremony, to the local chapter of the United Daughters of the Confederacy, so they could preserve it for posterity. The recording was later transferred to the national headquarters of the UDC in Richmond, where it resided for many years....But, like the Alexander recording, its story was far from finished.

A number of sources have referred to the UDC recording as being a wax cylinder. If they are referring to the mysterious Florida recording from circa 1898, it was undoubtedly a wax cylinder. However, if they are referring to the equally mysterious 1932 New Orleans recording or the 1934 Simmons recording, as well as the 1935 Alexander recording, they are incorrect. By the mid-1930s cylinders had long since gone by the wayside in favor of the thick discs. Plus, in recent times, the UDC/Simmons recording has been verified as being a wax disc. This "cylinder/disc" confusion will play a part in the next phase of the story.

CHAPTER 12

Recorded Versions of the Rebel Yell—Part III: The UDC and the Museum of the Confederacy

Audio Recordings—Continued

For a number of years few people were even aware of the existence of the UDC disc; as time passed, it was nearly forgotten altogether. But as interest in the Civil War was occasionally revitalized by events like the centennial of the War in the 1960s and Ken Burns' PBS documentary in the 1990s, interest in the Rebel Yell had a rebirth as well. When researchers started poking around it didn't take long for the story of the UDC recording to surface and people began trying to get access to it. This turned out to be a frustrating and difficult task.

Various people through the years made unsuccessful attempts to gain access to the recording. In the last twenty-five years at least three major efforts have been made to achieve some sort of inroad to the situation. The problem seemed to revolve around the UDC ladies guarding their various treasures, including the recording, very closely. It had apparently become somewhat of an icon for them and they feared having it lost, stolen or damaged...which was a reasonable concern. The trouble with this protective philosophy was that the disc had little intrinsic worth as an object; its value lay in what was purportedly on it, and if that wasn't recovered and proven, then it was essentially worthless.

In the mid-1980s historian and Yell enthusiast, Monte Akers, attempted, in a series of phone calls, to get permission to at least hear the recording. Of course, he ultimately hoped to get an okay to make a copy of it. His efforts met with little result, except for an acknowledgement of the recording's existence. Phone calls were not returned, and he never actually felt that he had ever been in contact with anyone who had the necessary authority to approve or deny his request.

Not being one to give up easily, Akers tried again in the late 1990s, this time enlisting the help of a fellow Yell researcher to make what he called "a two-pronged assault on the UDC." The ladies, unfortunately, proved just as persistent in their denial of permission as Akers was in his attempt to acquire it. So, once again, he had similar results. This time, in addition to acknowledging their possession of the recording, they went a little further and said they had no equipment to play the wax cylinder on, even if they wanted to let him listen to it. Akers then made offers to locate the necessary equipment in order to have a chance to hear the recording. Once again, the ladies didn't respond to his overtures.—At the end of his odyssey, Monte Akers, with some frustration, concluded; "They do not seem anxious to share what they 'preserved for posterity' with those of us who make-up that posterity."

Now, the UDC ladies' statement about not having the proper equipment on which to play the wax cylinder brings up several questions and at least one intriguing possibility.— Since we now know that the Simmons recording is on a wax disc, what were the ladies referring to? Did the contact people involved simply misspeak, or make some mistake of memory? Is it possible the error occurred because they didn't actually have much direct, firsthand knowledge of the recording? Is it even possible they were merely saying that they didn't have a record player on the premises? That seems unlikely and, at any rate, a small problem to overcome.— The door that is left open here is that we are talking about two (or three) different recordings! The various attempts to hear the recording were primarily directed at the Simmons recording, while the ladies may have been referring to the Florida recording, which, if it exists, would have been on a wax cylinder. If that's the case, it is indeed unlikely they would have possessed the needed equipment, and it means there may still be hope, however remote, of recovering that lone remaining jewel. If the 1932 New Orleans recording exists, it may turn up someday as well.

Now we need to fast forward to 2004 and introduce a fellow named S. Waite Rawls III, who is the executive director of the Museum of the Confederacy in Richmond. In that year Rawls attended a Civil War Preservation Trust meeting in Wilmington, North Carolina and heard the 1935 Alexander recording for the first time; it kindled his interest in the Rebel Yell and set him on a path of discovery.

With his ultimate goal being an audio CD of and about the Yell, he had to decide how to proceed. Realizing that one man hollering the Rebel Yell (however authentic) was far from what was actually heard during battle, Rawls made the same decision that Don Bracken was making at about the same time. Quite independently from one another they got sound technicians involved using similar processes. Like Bracken's recording I described earlier, Rawls had his people use computer technology to multiply and vary the single voice on the Alexander recording. They repeatedly looped it over itself, each time making minor changes in volume, bass and treble, until they had emulated a company of approximately 70 soldiers, the same size unit as the Bracken recording.

The results from both these projects were terrific; Bracken, Rawls and their compatriots are all to be commended for their efforts. I have heard both recordings and they are remarkably similar. With these recordings we are getting very near our goal, plus, after hearing them, it is becoming increasingly clear why the Yell so unnerved and provoked fear in the Union troops.

From this point forward, Rawls took a few extra steps in his quest, and along the way accomplished a minor miracle. He was pleased with his new "unit" recording, but had some qualms about releasing an audio CD with only the one source on which to base it. So, he began looking for an additional source to help verify the one he already had.

To his surprise, he got wind of the Simmons/MGM recording that the UDC was holding in their archives right there in Richmond. This is exactly what he was looking for, and since the Museum of the Confederacy and the UDC National Headquarters have so much in common, are in the same city and cooperate with each other on projects, he assumed it wouldn't be a problem getting his hands on the recording....Wrong!

Once again, the ladies of the UDC voiced the same litany of concerns they had given to everyone else. I assume Rawls used his Southern charm, his position with the museum and the fact he was known to them to help him prevail in this stalemate....No luck! Finally, in desperation, he appealed to their reason with the "intrinsic value" argument stated above: "Look, the wax itself is worth nothing unless the sound is what it is [supposed to be]."—These were the magic words which finally, miraculously released the treasure! The UDC agreed to let Rawls take the old disc and attempt to recover the sound from it. He took it to a high tech studio in order to get the best quality sound and ensure the safety of the recording.

Rawls didn't know what to expect when the studio delivered the CD of the sound they'd captured from the old wax. Would it sound similar to the other recording? Would it be completely different? If different, what would that imply? Would we again have little idea for certain what the Yell sounded like, or are we looking at multiple versions, or, put simply, just what do we have here?—As it turned out, there was nothing to worry about. Rawls said, "I put it in a boom box and–son of a gun–it sounded exactly the same."

With this confirmation, the audio CD was now a definite full-speed-ahead project. A script was written, music selected and, most importantly of all, a considerable amount of studio/computer time was spent further manipulating the two recordings. They were digitally remastered, then the two different Yells were combined, and the same techniques which had been used earlier were then applied to increase the "head-count" in order to simulate larger groups of soldiers.

On the finished CD, entitled *The Rebel Yell Lives!*, both the Alexander and Simmons solo recordings are heard, and they do bear a remarkable resemblance to one another. Scott C. Boyd, in an article for the April, 2009 edition of the *Civil War News* said, "Both have a high-pitched, shrieking, animalistic quality."

The first unit simulation is a new version of a company of 70 men. This is followed by a regiment of 500 Rebels, then a brigade of 1800 soldiers, and finally with thousands-upon-thousands of Confederates of the Army of Northern Virginia hollering the Rebel Yell up and down the line.— What is heard on these tracks is quite amazing. Listening to them, it becomes instantly understandable why the sound, the effect on both friend and foe, and the reputation of the Rebel Yell have become the stuff of legend.

The CD includes some interesting commentary tracks; the music on the first track is Richard Bales' *Dixie* from *The Confederacy*, and the final musical track is *Dixie* as conducted by Arturo Toscanini. These are the two pieces that were mentioned earlier; I said that I would provide a better alternative source for these recordings, and this is it! The new audio CD, *The Rebel Yell Lives!*, can currently be purchased through the Museum of the Confederacy (see Appendix B). In the near future it should be available through other sources as well.

Thanks to the efforts and persistence of people such as Monte Akers, Don Bracken and S. Waite Rawls III, and with the issuing of this CD, we have, at last, found the "Holy Grail" of the Rebel Yell. This may well prove to be the final word on the subject of the recorded Yell, unless some totally unknown and unexpected new information should suddenly turn up in history's musty attic.

The discovery of a bona fide version of the Yell does not, however, mean that there aren't a number of other interesting aspects of the Rebel Yell to investigate, and many wonderful stories about it to be told....So, let's proceed ahead and see what else we can find.

PART III: STORIES, POEMS, ETC.

CHAPTER 13

The First and Last Rebel Yells: Mountain Boomers, Uncle Hade and the REA

The First

It can be difficult to distinguish between some "origination" stories and "first usage" stories; they seem to become intertwined, carrying some aspects of both. I tend to draw the line in the following manor: Any antebellum Yell story is part of the origins history, while any early War Yell story would be first usage history. But, even with this guideline, it can still be hard to untangle one from the other.

Company D of the 7th Virginia Infantry (known as the "Mountain Boomers") was from Giles County, Virginia in the Southwestern part of the state. Most of its members had enlisted at Giles Courthouse between May and July, 1861. This unit claims to have "originated" the Rebel Yell while in training in Giles County.

The story goes that during a training session they accidently let loose with a blood-curdling yell, which they apparently liked and decided to adopt as part of the unit's identity. As it was passed around and imitated by other units it became a sort of "standard issue" yell used by all Confederate soldiers.

However likely or unlikely the above story may be, there is little question that one candidate for being the first Yell does have some claim to legitimacy. This is due in part to the fact that it was during the first major battle of the War, First Manassas (Bull Run). The timing alone gives the claim some weight. In addition, some of the earliest accounts of the Yell were given in connection with this battle.

As related earlier in chapter 8, during a portion of the battle known as the attack at Henry House Hill the order was given by Jackson to "yell like furies" as his men made a bayonet charge.—Also at Bull Run it was reported, apparently by a Union soldier, that General Beauregard's troops emitted an "unearthly wail" during their battle charge.—Ultimately, the Federal forces were sent retreating back to Washington D.C. in the famous "Great Skedaddle" and this early use of the Rebel Yell was thought to have played an important role in the Confederate victory.

In his book, *The Blazing Southwest*, Paul Wellman claims that the Rebel Yell was first used in the "Texas War of Independence," making it an origin story, except for the confusing complication that that war was also a war of rebellion; the Texans were rebels against Mexico. Does this give it the right to be called the Rebel Yell? Whatever you may choose to believe, Wellman says it was this yell that was introduced by the Texans to the rest of the Confederate Army.

The best possible argument for this to be a first usage story or, at least, an early usage story, is the Battle of Wilson's Creek in Southwestern Missouri. This battle is generally acknowledged to be the second major battle of the War and had a large Texas component under the command of General Ben McCullough. The result here was another Confederate victory; whether the Texans' "War of Independence" Rebel Yell had a significant role in the battle isn't clear.—Also of note in this battle is the early Native American influence on the Yell. As previously mentioned, they were small in number, but contributed greatly to the nature and use of the Rebel Yell at Wilson's Creek (see chapter 6).

The Last

There are a number of ways to consider what the "last Rebel Yell" might be.—Was it the last one screeched during battle? Was it the final one uttered under any condition near the War's end? Could it be more personal, such as the last time an individual soldier or ex-soldier gave the

Yell before his death? Might it be the last opportunity for someone to hear (or record) an authentic Yell?—All of these, as well as others, could qualify as being candidates for the last Rebel Yell; they fulfill some concept of what that phrase might mean.

Without doubt, there are many claimants in the first of these categories. The final battles fought in the East, West and Trans-Mississippi all had versions of the Rebel Yell splitting the air to the very end. To cite one battle, unit or individual as having the honor of being "the last" is essentially impossible. The same can be said for the other categories as well. What it basically comes down to are the stories connected with each; they are what breathe life into any aspect of history. And there are some wonderful ones to relate on this topic.

In a 1905 issue of *Confederate Veteran* magazine an ex-soldier from Kentucky, H.K. Nelson, originally from Tennessee during the War, writes an article in which he has a nomination for the last Rebel Yell.—At the end of the War he was headed home with a group comprised of surrendered Confederates from six or seven consolidated regiments. Every fourth man had been allowed to kept a rifle for the group's general protection and well being, and they had managed to save one regimental flag, furled and under cover. From this point forward, let Nelson tell the story:

> I have read and heard a good deal about 'the last shot fired,' 'the last man killed,' and 'the last charge' made by Confederate soldiers, but I've never yet seen any account of the last 'Rebel yell.' As no one seems to claim this distinction, I modestly suggest that it be allowed to a crowd of us Tennesseans who were returning home, after our surrender at Greensboro, N.C., through the western portion of that State and East Tennessee....
>
> When we were nearing the little Rebel town of Asheville (North Carolina), the flag was unfurled, the ranks 'dressed,' and, placing our men with guns at 'right shoulder shift' in front, we prepared to make our last military display, notwithstanding the town was in the hands of the Federals...I

do remember as distinctly as if it happened yesterday that just as we were passing a cottage the command, for some purpose, was halted. Standing on the stile leading into the yard of the cottage, on the right-hand side of the street were three ladies within easy reach of our color bearer, who was standing within a few feet of me. One of these ladies was very enthusiastic, and had been speaking encouragingly to the boys as they passed by. Turning to the ensign, she said: 'Let me put my hands on that flag.' He drooped it over her head, and she caught it in her hands, kissed it, and rubbed it over her face; then, with tears in her eyes, she said: 'Carry it to your home in triumph. It is not yet disgraced, nor has it been trailed in the dust.' As she finished speaking a Federal sergeant with a file of men came up and informed her that the provost marshal requested her to report at his headquarters immediately. Drawing herself up with the dignity of a queen, and the tears still shining in her eyes, she motioned him away with her hand and said: 'Tell your provost marshal I have no use for either him or his headquarters.' Whether he had orders for her arrest or not, I do not know; but he turned at once and marched away. Then went up the old 'Rebel yell,' the last mother's son of us giving tongue loud and long. It was not exactly in tone with the old fighting yell, yet it was one of triumph, and I think it entitles our little squad of paroled prisoners to the honor of giving for the last time our significant 'Rebel yell.' I've often thought of that true and plucky daughter of Dixie and wonder if she is yet living.

Few could argue with the sheer, heartfelt emotion of this story, no matter how one might view the validity of the claim for being the last Rebel Yell.

On the morning of Saturday, September 24, 1864 a large band of Missouri guerillas under the command of William "Bloody Bill" Anderson entered the Central Missouri town of Fayette, which was under Federal command. As they were disguised wearing blue uniforms, the Rebels made it to the center of town before the chaos of battle erupted.

The two Union strongholds were the courthouse in town and a permanent encampment with blockhouses on the north edge of town. Both of these positions were nearly impregnable to an attack by men on horseback carrying pistols. Nevertheless, the guerillas divided their forces and attacked both locations. It was not a wise decision and would prove to be the worst defeat under Anderson's leadership.

During the twin battles a guerilla named Garrett M. Groomer, who belonged to George Todd's company, seeing the futility of the situation pulled two pistols out of his "guerilla shirt," dismounted from his horse and charged the heavy door, firing both weapons and, according to witnesses, screaming the Rebel Yell all the way until he was shot dead by Yankee bullets.

In some versions of the story the "heavy door" he charged belonged to the courthouse and he was the "mysterious red-bearded man" many saw attacking the building singlehandedly. In other versions, the door he charged was on one of the blockhouses at the encampment to the north.

Either way, Garrett Groomer gave what was definitely, for him, his last Rebel Yell as he charged and fired in frustration.

On Tuesday, November 12, 1929 the Laurel, Mississippi newspaper, *The Morning Call*, ran the following headlines and story about another type of last Rebel Yell:

THRILL OF "DIXIE" IS FATAL TO AGED VETERAN
Last Breath Was Given To Battle-cry Of Lost Cause
Confederate Veteran Cheering When Fatal Stroke Comes

Beauvoir (Mississippi) Nov. 11—F.R. Goodrum, 80-year old Confederate veteran, fell dead on the porch of the Jefferson Davis Soldiers Home here this afternoon at four o'clock just after he had raised his gray hat high above his head and had yelled the old rebel cry he had learned in the sixties. The old veteran was cheering his war-time tune, "Dixie", when he died.

The Knights Templar Band, Jaques De Molay Commandery Number 2, of New Orleans, had been playing concert music all day for the old veterans when at four o'clock the band leader, as a fitting finale to the day's entertainment, gave orders to his musicians to strike up the old battle tune of the South.

In a moment the first clear notes of the well loved "Dixie" floated across the porch of the Soldiers Home where a little band of the wearers of the gray were sitting listening to the music. Every one of them arose to his feet and cheered the battle song. The rebel yell once more rang out from their throats as it had done at Chancersville [sic], at Malvern Hill and at Gettysburg.

The excitement of the old veterans was great but it was too much for Goodrum. He was waving his hat high above his head and was cheering at the top of his voice but of a sudden his hat fell from his hand, the cheering stilled in his throat, he stood unsteady for a fraction of a second and toppled over into a heap on the floor of the porch. He was dead before aid could be summoned.

The dead soldier's home was in Vicksburg. Funeral arrangements have not yet been made but it is likely that he will be buried near his old home in that city.

Without question, it can be declared that this tale is indeed about F.R. Goodrum's last Rebel Yell; and a fitting finale it was for his life...in his home state, surrounded by his comrades, with a band playing *Dixie* and the Rebel Yell on his tongue!

The final chapter in Frank X. Tolbert's book, *An Informal History of Texas*, is called, "Hunting for the Last Rebel Yell." It's a marvelous story in which Tolbert relates how in the spring of 1949 he took a tape recorder and went searching for the last four Southern veterans still surviving in Texas, hoping to capture what he'd "...been told was the most fearsome sound ever uttered by man—the Rebel yell of the Confederate army."

Since each of these men was already over a hundred years old, he knew time was of the essence.

First he went to Bonham to visit with 103-year-old Joseph Haden Whitsett, who was better known as "Uncle Hade." When informed of the reason for Tolbert's visit, Uncle Hade said, "'Can't do it....Can't Rebel yell. I'm sorry. I tried to learn it a thousand times when I was with Shelby's Escort (General Joseph Shelby) during the war. I didn't seem to

have the right kind of a voice. Wish you could have heard
General Joe, himself, Rebel yell. He could make a full-voiced
loafer wolf sound like someone blowing on a penny whistle.'"

"'I can't do you no Rebel yell,' said Whitsett, 'but I'll sing
into your gadget.'

"He sang in a cracked baritone that had once been a good
voice:

> 'Hide that mule!
> Old Joe Shelby's at the door.
> He'll take your mule
> And ride him till his back is sore.'

"The old man commented: 'General Joe didn't like the
words to that song much.'"

Next Tolbert drove to Robertson County to see an old
veteran named, Walter Washington Williams. When he
located Williams, sitting out on his porch and posed
the question about the Rebel Yell to him, Tolbert was
disappointed to hear the answer.

"'Used to could do it. But I haven't got the throat linings
for it now. When you get a hundred seven you can't do
everything you want to no more.'

"He said he was about to give up fox hunting 'and it's a
pity for I must be the oldest fox hunter in the world. I can
still sit here and listen to the dogs running fox off in the
woods.'"

After a few cordialities, Tolbert took his leave and headed
to Wichita Falls where he was to interview Thomas E.
Riddle, age 104.

In his youth Riddle had been a courier on General
Robert E. Lee's staff. At the time of Tolbert's visit he had
just divorced his third wife, whose transgressions included
the fact she had torn up his favorite picture of General Lee.

Finally, after visiting for awhile, came the question: "'Can
you do the Rebel Yell?'"

"'No, sir, I can't do the Rebel yell—not any more. Not
rightly anyway. I remember hearing it the best at Gettysburg
and in the Wilderness. It was a terrible sound. But I can't do

it rightly any more. No old man can. It's a young man's yell. For those seventy or under. You won't find a man on earth today who can do it rightly.'"

At this point, Tolbert was beginning to believe Riddle's parting remark; he only had one ex-Confederate left. In Franklin County, 103-year-old Samuel Merrill Raney was his last hope.

He found Raney sitting outside on a hot day wearing a heavy sweater and a stocking cap. Tolbert introduced himself and told the old man that he was from Dallas.

Raney replied, "'Last time I was in Dallas it was full of carpetbaggers. Hear it still is.'"

Later the old veteran's youngest son, 75-year-old George, came in from the fields, and after some pleasantries said, "'Papa was a field music [sic] in the States War. He's still got some flutes.'"

"Mr. Raney said: 'I was a fighting soldier too. I didn't get in the band until toward the last.'"

The "fighting soldier" remark was Tolbert's cue to ask the Rebel Yell question one last time…."'Can you do the Rebel yell?'"

The son, George, answered: "'Papa can. But he best not. The last time he done it, it was seven years ago, I think. And he got a coughing fit after he done it. He best not.'"

Then Samuel Raney began to reminisce about "the War." How he'd been sixteen when he joined in 1862 and how he'd seen his first action at Murfreesboro. How the cedar trees and cotton stalks had been set on fire by the cannons when his unit charged….

"Abruptly the old man threw back his face, opened his beard-rimmed mouth, and started yelling like an opera singer hitting almost impossibly high notes. It was a little like an angry elephant's scream. There was a main cry and then a sort of falsetto echo back of the main cry. It was as if a mountain lion and a coyote were crying in chorus—if the lion and the coyote had bass voices."

As the Yell became a convulsion of coughs, George ran to the well for a dipper of water and Tolbert ran to his car for his tape recorder. When he returned the old man was drinking water and feeling much better. Tolbert showed them the recorder and explained how he would make a permanent record of the Yell, just as soon as the old veteran felt up to doing it again, and the recorder was plugged in.

"'We haven't got no electricity,' said George Raney. 'We never did tie on to REA.'"

Tolbert offered to take them to the nearest house that did have electricity, but discovered that the old man didn't ever ride in cars; it bothered his kidneys. Then George said he thought it would be best if "Papa" didn't yell again for a few days.

"'You come back later and bring a battery for that talking machine and he'll yell for you.'"

Some days later, when Tolbert returned to Franklin County with a battery-powered tape recorder, Samuel Raney wasn't sitting outside as before. After knocking on the door and calling out several times, George Raney came in from the field and said:

"'Papa died.'

"Probably the Rebel yell died with him."

While subsequent recorded discoveries have eased some of the dark irony inherent in this story, it is still one of my favorite "last Rebel Yell" stories, and I would urge the reader to locate a copy of Tolbert's book and read the complete, unabridged chapter as it appears there.

CHAPTER 14

The Yankee Cheer:
Hoo-rays, Hurrahs and Huzzas

Having discussed the Rebel Yell long and hard, with more yet to come, it only seems fair to devote a little time and space to the Northern variety battle cry. We primarily need to note how it differs from the Rebel Yell and if any similarities exist between the two. Of course, we'll try to cover origins and some interesting stories as well.

As indicated earlier in this book and by the current chapter title, the Federal troops employed what can be more correctly called "a cheer." As usual, this is a blanket statement which does have some exceptions and even differences of opinion involved with it.

The concept of an organized military cheer is undoubtedly an ancient one. It certainly has a long history throughout the centuries in Europe, and that is where our focus should be. Given the nature of the Northern population at the time of the Civil War and how it was reflected in the makeup of the army, there were indeed strong European traditions at work. Those of Germany and England are of particular interest.

While German people had been coming to America for many decades, there was a particularly large influx in the twenty years preceding the Civil War. These new emigrants were fleeing from a series of German Civil Wars; some merely to escape the terror, while others came to America after finding themselves on the losing side of a particular conflict. They brought with them a long Germanic military history which included the disciplined shouts and cheers they were accustomed to in the old country.

Likewise, the English had a similar military tradition which they brought with them, and which had been on display for the previous hundred years in the French and Indian War, the Revolutionary War, the War of 1812 and most recently the Mexican War. Their military history also included various "set" cheers for different occasions, including a charge into battle.—Arthur Freemantle, an English officer observing the War, remarked, "The Southern troops...always yell in a manner peculiar to themselves. The Yankee cheer is much more like ours..."

Many of the Irish who had arrived in America through the decades had followed the familiar Celtic path to the mountains, the South and the new West across the Mississippi River. However, included in the new Northern amalgam were the more recently arrived Irish, who had flocked to the big cities of the North following the hunger and poverty of the potato famine at home. By the time of the Civil War these various traditions, along with others, had merged into a melting pot of ideas and styles.

This coalescence of traditions included what became the cheers and shouts of the new Northern army.

The most common descriptions of the Federal cheer (usually given by Northern soldiers) called it deep in tone, hearty and manly in nature and measured in execution. This was quite opposite to their view of the Rebel Yell—A Union soldier, Henry Tremain, who was obviously proud of the shouts of General Crook's army, in which he served, referred degradingly to the Rebel Yell as "their peculiar faint cheer."—Another Federal soldier, Newton Kirk, said, "The shrill yells of the Rebels, mingled with the hoarser cheers of our own men."—George T. Stevens, also a Yankee soldier, spoke of "The vigorous manly cheers of the Northern soldiers, so different from the shrill yell of the Rebels."—A Northern engineer named Sam Bradbury thought the Rebel Yell "...sounds like a lot of school boys just let loose."— Yet another Federal soldier, Gilbert Hays, cited earlier (see chapter 9), was in agreement with Bradbury, but held the Rebel Yell in higher esteem:

The peculiarity of the rebel yell is worthy of mention, but

none of the old soldiers who heard it once will ever forget it. Instead of the deep-chested manly cheer of the Union men, the rebel yell was a falsetto yelp which, when heard at a distance, reminded one of a lot of school boys at play. It was a peculiar affair for a battle yell, but though we made fun of it at first, we grew to respect it before the war is over. The yell might sound effeminate, but those who uttered it were not effeminate by any means. When the Union men charged, it was heads erect, shoulders squared and thrown back, and with a firm stride, but when the Johnnies charged, it was with a jog trot in a half bent position, and though they might be met with heavy and blighting volleys, they came on with the pertinacity of bulldogs, filling up gaps and trotting on with their never-ceasing 'ki-yi' until we found them face to face.

Yet another Yank, an infantryman from Pennsylvania, also had a feminine note in his observation that "when they got close enough they screamed that woman like scream and with fixed bayonet on they came."

The Southern view, as expressed by J. Harvie Dew, pointed out that in comparison "with that of the Confederate, [the Yankee Cheer] lacked in vigor, vocal breadth, pitch, and resonance. This was unquestionably attributable to the fact that the soldiery of the North was drawn and recruited chiefly from large cities and towns, from factory districts and from the more densely settled portions of the country." This was as opposed to the South where "Hollering, screaming, yelling...were familiar sounds throughout the farming districts...in the days gone by."— General Jubal "Old Jube" Early, the source of this volume's front quote, said that the yell of "the Confederate soldier... is never mistaken for the studied hurrahs of the Yankees."

The various word or phonetic versions of the Northern cheer all seem to have had a common ancestor, as they appear to be quite similar in nature. Jubal Early touched on it with his "studied hurrahs" comment above.

As has often been the case, we turn again to J. Harvie

Dew for some definitive explanations and examples of the Yankee Cheer. Again asserting the city background of many Northern soldiers, Dew says:

> When companies and regiments were formed in the beginning of the war and the men wished to cheer their captain or some higher officer, they had no alternative but to adopt the old method of proposing three cheers…'Hip, hip, hip' 'Hurrah, hurrah,' etc. Then later when in battle they attempted to yell, 'Hurrah, Hurrah!' but in the excitement of a charge the modification of tone and the haste of utterance produced, 'Hoo, ray, hoo, ray!' the first syllable pronounced with a short and quick note, the last with a higher and prolonged tone. Their 'Cheer,' as they called it, always sounded to me like…'Hey, hey, hey,' or 'Rey, rey, rey,' having about the same tone and sound. I rarely ever heard the first syllable….
>
> From what I have stated it is easy to see that the 'Rebel Yell' was the only true and unquestioned yell; and when hundreds or thousands of men, stimulated by the excitement and vigor of a charge, gave this yell in battle, it was demonical and demoralizing in the extreme.

In another article Dew stated, "'Hoo-ray! Hoo-ray! Hoo-ray!'… was intended for the word 'hurrah,' but that pronunciation I never heard in a charge….In many instances the yell seemed to be the simple interjection 'heigh,' rendered with the same tone which was given to 'ray.'"

J. Harvie Dew's opinion aside, many swear the Yankee Cheer was in fact a much practiced "Hurrah! Hurrah!" etc.—Still another variation given by veterans, and passed along by Dr. Bell Irvin Wiley, is a highly arranged "hip, hip, huzza, huzza, huzza"

It has been speculated that these various formulaic cheers have traveled in military channels through the years, from the Civil War until the present, and serve as predecessors to the United States Army's "hoo-hah" and the United States Marine Corps' "ooh-rah" which are in use today.

Of course, there are exceptions to every rule, and at least two of interest have surfaced concerning the Union cheer.

A sergeant from Massachusetts reported hearing an Irish brigade, led by General Meagher, doing a yell that sounded much like the Rebel Yell. While there are no known additional accounts to corroborate this story, it certainly doesn't seem too far fetched to be true. I would view it as the Celtic influence coming out once again, albeit from a somewhat unexpected direction.

Then we have a story about members of the 5th Minnesota Volunteer Infantry at the Battle of Iuka, Mississippi. It was reported that during the fighting they used what was termed "Indian War Cries" as they charged the Confederate line. It was additionally reported that this tactic "scared the hell out of the Southern soldiers" because it caught them so unawares. Once again, there is no corroboration for this incident.

If either, or both, of the above stories are accurate I suppose we should file them under: "Johnny Reb gets a taste of his own medicine!"

CHAPTER 15

Miscellaneous Stories, Articles and Quotes: Molly Cottontail and Little Sorrel

In relating the information in the preceding chapters a great many quotes were taken from lengthier writings. What was edited out was because it was not immediately pertinent to the subject at hand, and not because it was uninteresting material. Other items of interest simply didn't find their way into one of the other chapters for a variety of reasons. Many of these are worthy of inclusion at either full or greater length, as are a number of shorter, but pertinent, quotes not previously included. This chapter will be devoted to correcting that situation.

The article which follows, and from which some excerpts have previously appeared, was originally delivered as an impromptu speech in 1891 at a Confederate Reunion in Memphis. It was later refined into an article for the Memphis *Appeal*, and reprinted twice in the Confederate Veteran magazine in 1893 and 1905. The author is Colonel Kellar Anderson of the 1st Kentucky, better known as the Kentucky Orphan Brigade The unit received the name because of the status of their home state, which was in Federal control. They couldn't return home for the course of the War, their supply lines from Kentucky were non-existent and they received little help from other Confederate sources.—At the reunion in Memphis, the widow of a famous Southern naval officer, who was seated on the dais, expressed a desire to hear the Rebel Yell again. The old veterans in attendance did their best to accommodate her wish, and then Kellar Anderson took the podium:

> There is a Southern mother on this stand who says she wants to hear 'the Rebel yell' once more.

The announcement transforms, and in an instant I find myself acting the humble part of file-closer to Company I, 5th Kentucky Infantry....

It is nearing sunset; and after two days of fearful carnage... the enemy has been driven pell-mell from many parts of the field....The sulphurous smoke has increased until almost stifling. Only fifty yards of space separates us from the gallant Mississippians we are there to support. They have clung to the ridge with a deathlike grip, but their last cartridge has been fired at the enemy, and, their support being at hand, these sturdy soldiers of Longstreet's Corps are ordered to retire.

Simultaneously the support was ordered forward. As the Mississippians retired the deep-volumed shouts of the enemy told us plainer than could words that the enemy thought they had routed them. O, how differently we regarded the situation! If they could have seen them as we...ranging themselves in columns of files behind large trees to enable us to get at the enemy with an unbroken front, each man as we passed throwing cap high...in honor of our presence— then I imagine their shouts would have been suppressed. 'Steady in the center! Hold your fire! Hold the colors back!' The center advanced too rapidly. We are clear of our friends now, only the enemy in front, and we meet face to face on a spur of Mission Ridge...and we are separated by eighty yards. Thud! And down goes Private Robertson. He turned, smiled, and died. Thud! Corporal Gray shot through the neck...Thud! Thud! Thud! The fallen increase, and are to be counted by the hundreds. 'Forward! Forward!' rang out along the line. We move slowly to the front.

There are now sixty yards between us....We have all that is possible for human to bear; our losses are fearful, and each moment some comrade passes to the unknown....I feel a shock about my left breast, spin like a top in the air, and comedown in a heap. I know not how long before came the sounds, 'Forward! Forward! Forward!' I rise on my elbow. Look! Look! There they go, all at breakneck speed, the bayonet at charge. The firing appears to suddenly cease for about five seconds. Then arose that do-or-die expression, that maniacal maelstrom of sound; that penetrating, rasping, shrieking, blood-curdling noise that could be heard for miles on earth and whose volume reached the heavens, such an expression as never yet came from the throats of sane men, but from men whom the searing blast of an imaginary hell would not check while the sound lasted.

The Battle of Chickamauga is won....

Dear Southern mother, that was 'the Rebel yell,' and only such scenes ever did or ever will produce it.

Even when engaged, that expression from the Confederate soldier always made my hair stand on end. The young men and youths who composed this unearthly music were lusty, jolly, clear-voiced, hardened soldiers, full of courage and proud to march in rags, barefoot, dirty and hungry, with head erect, to meet the plethoric ranks of the best-equipped and best-fed army of modern times. Alas! Now many of them are decrepit from ailment and age! And, although we will never grow old enough to cease being proud of the record of the Confederate soldier and the dear old mothers who bore them, we can never again, even at your bidding, dear, dear mother, produce 'the Rebel yell.' Never again; never, never, never.

In a 1913 volume of the *Confederate Veteran* magazine a veteran named Alexander Hunter, originally from Virginia, living at the time in Washington, D.C. contributed an article which actually had two separate stories in one, both concerning the Rebel Yell:

I heard the Rebel yell in a modified form when Lee's army was in winter quarters at Gurney's Station, near Fredericksburg....It was a bright, warm day in January, although forty-eight hours previously it had snowed steadily, and the earth was covered with its fleecy mantle knee-deep.

About noon the men of Longstreet's old brigade...were summoned from their tents by a most unwonted uproar; and seeing a cloud of skirmishers lead the way, they fired the snowballs as if each man were the prize pitcher of a crack baseball team. The men caught on and fell into line with greater alacrity than they ever did before. It was time to be on the jump, for it was not a minute before the soldiers were steadied in line of battle and had molded an armful of snowballs before the Texans were upon us. They came cheering and hallooing, and their onset swept us away. Those who were not rolling in the snow for the rear; and once out of gunshot distance, they went to work getting in a fresh supply of ammunition, waiting for their chance. It soon came. A loud shout, and Pickett's Brigade caught Hood's on the flank and doubled them up; and while Pickett's men were screaming 'Victory!' a fresh brigade struck them in the rear, and they went to pieces. Soon there was great cheering by thousands of voices, but it was mere shouting, not the Rebel yell.

*****

Though in many battles, I never but once noticed it particularly, for as one of the performers I was struck with my own performance and did not notice others' efforts.

On the fateful day, the 31st of August, 1862, Longstreet had gotten through Thoroughfare Gap and formed his men in a double line of battle about half a mile in length....In our front the Federal infantry came surging toward us, uttering the measured hurrahs that had neither sentiment nor music, and the sound had no sinister meaning to any 'grayback' on that field...and the ground quivered, the air grew murky from musketry fire, while the white smoke of the cannon made a faint fog that made things unreal.

Suddenly the hurrahs of the enemy were plainly heard. They were in a depression of the ground, and when they emerged a few hundreds of yards distant they came sweeping upon us in grand style....We swept onward, driving back their first line and making for a six-gun battery. They poured grape and canister into us, making many a gap....Our line, ragged and torn, surged forward, but we could go no farther. The enemy's reserves came up and broke our line into scattered fragments. But we rallied and the Rebel yell commenced as we sprang forward. I could not gauge its swell or volume. Just at this juncture I was wounded in the arm, my musket dropped from my hand, and then I leaned against one of the captured guns and took a survey of the scene....

It was at this time that our second line started across that storm-swept plain....

It was a hurly-burly of fire, flame, smoke, and dust. When our reserve, led by Hood's Texas Brigade, the pride and glory of the Army of Northern Virginia, came on a run, gathering up all the fragments of the other commands in their front, and this second line dashed straight at the enemy, then I heard the Rebel yell with all its appalling significance.

It was growing late, the sun was low in the west, and before me was the most superlative scene of grandeur my eyes ever rested upon....It was the very acme of 'glorious war'...and the supreme hour had come.

Pope had resolved to 'make or break,' and piled in all his reserves in one mighty effort to sweep the field. The federals advanced, it seemed, with the resistless power of an avalanche, and with their hurrahs, the belching of the cannon, the rattling of the musketry a commotion was made that seemed to fill the world with turmoil; but higher, shriller, clearer above all rose the Rebel yell. I never in my life heard such a fearsome, awful sound. The Federal officers spoke by the card when they said that in many instances this yell caused their ranks to break before the Rebel charge was made.

The Rebel yell as I heard it that evening while leaning against the cannon made a lifelong impression on me. I have often dreamed of it; above the uproar of a great battle it dominated. On those charging columns of blue it had a decided effect, for it portended capture, mutilation, or death and brought eternity very near.

The preceding two articles, each simply titled, "The Rebel Yell," have a couple of other things in common. First, they are both well written, literate and expressive. Second, the two authors had the same experience of being wounded in battle, and only then, when forced to stop their charge, did they truly hear, appreciate and understand the effect and significance of the Rebel Yell.

After the Battle of the Wilderness, late in the day, as the armies of Lee and Grant sat in their trenches a shouting match of sorts developed between the two sides. First the North gave a Union cheer and then the Army of Northern Virginia came back with the Rebel Yell. Douglas Southall Freeman described it as follows:

Confident and rejoicing, they raised the rebel yell in Anderson's corps and took it up all along the whole line. At a given point, one could hear it on the right, then in front and than dying away in the distance on the left. 'Again the shout arose on the right—again it rushed down upon us from a distance of perhaps two miles,' one officer wrote,— 'again we caught it and flung it joyously to the left, where it ceased only when the last post had huzzahed. The effect was beyond expression...It seemed to fill every heart with new life, to inspire every nerve with might never known before. Men seemed fairly convulsed with the fierce enthusiasm and I believe that if at that instant the advance of the whole army upon Grant could have been ordered, we should have swept him into the very Rappahannock.'

In an article titled, "The So-called Rebel Yell," which appeared in a 1927 issue of the *Confederate Veteran* magazine, the writer, W. A. Love, of Columbus, Mississippi gave the facts about the Rebel Yell as he saw them. In most instances his views serve as reinforcement for ideas that have been previously explored:

As time passes and survivors of the war of 1861-1865, both Union and Confederate, continue to consciously or unconsciously miscall the term, 'Rebel Yell,' it is considered appropriate in the interest of historical accuracy to offer a suggestion as to its origin, purpose, and probable true acceptance. It was doubtless in its genesis devoid of any relation to an armed and opposing enemy.

Lord Fairfax, George Washington, and other early Virginia fox hunters were perhaps the first to introduce the yell as a means of encouragement to their dogs and the result of personal enthusiasm in the chase.

As immigration came South, Mississippi hunters brought it with them, or adopted it, for a like purpose, and, when the game was up, gave such vent to their excitement and enthusiasm as to make the welkin ring.

Nor was the custom confined to the grown-up deer and fox hunters, but the boy that didn't yell when he jumped a rabbit was considered somewhat unsportsmanlike and poky. Even to-day...woe to the Molly Cottontail that doesn't run low and fast...while the rabbit yell is sounding and the cur dogs are barking.

On April 30, 1861, the Prairie Guards, a military organization that became Company E, of the 11th Mississippi

Infantry, entrained at Crawford for the seat of war. As the train pulled out a young volunteer thrust himself half way out a window of the coach and gave a most thrilling yell, not of defiance and fight, but of enthusiasm; and, later, upon the sanguinary fields of Virginia, Maryland, and Pennsylvania, he gave the same, more vigorously if possible; but it was then called the 'Rebel Yell.'

Of course, it is impossible to describe the sound, individually or collectively given, but there is a vast difference...with the rebel yell of thousands of earnest and excited men determined to meet and drive back the enemy at all hazard.

But it was not on the battle field alone that the yell was heard, and they were all alike. Any occurrence out of the ordinary, or the appearance of a popular general offered an occasion which was generally improved....

So then, in the early days the yell was not given to scare the game, but to encourage the dogs, but during the war period, however, it was perhaps used both to scare the enemy and encourage the charging battle lines.

Yet it was not special encouragement that the Confederate soldiers needed, but rather men, guns, and ammunition to successfully defend their country, homes, and firesides.

In a short piece appearing in the *Confederate Veteran* magazine in 1910 under the heading, "Ohio Veteran Doesn't Like the 'Rebel Yell,'" ex-Union soldier William H. Morris, Company B, 10th O.V.C., Sunbury, Ohio asks if he can have a little space in the "Veteran" to make some corrections in a article written by a man named Ulmer, which he had read sometime the previous year. After proceeding point by point to make his corrections he gets to his final request: "I do not write this for the purpose of causing ill will. Brother Ulmer saw only one side. For Heaven's sake, do not give me the Rebel yell, for it used to give me the cold chills. I close with best wishes to all the Confederates."

The English officer, Arthur Freemantle, stated, "The Confederate officers declare that the Rebel yell has a particular merit, and always produces a salutary and useful effect upon their adversaries. A Corps is sometimes spoken of as a 'good yelling' regiment."

Another source speculates, "It is possible Confederate rebels adopted this practice in order to create the impression of a much larger force. Others suggest that certain Confederate regiments were especially good at delivering a convincing Rebel Yell, so they were often deployed as advance troops before a major engagement."—This line of thought seems to fall in well with the final statement above made by Freemantle. (See chapter 1.)

Dr. Bell Irvin Wiley wrote the following:

The primary function of the rousing yell was the relief of the shouter. As one Reb observed after a fight in 1864, 'I always said if I ever went on a charge, I wouldn't holler! But the very first time I fired off my gun I hollered as loud as I could, and I hollered every breath till we stopped.' At first there was no intention of inspiring terror in the enemy, but the practice soon attained such a reputation as a demoralizing agent that men were encouraged by their officers to shout as they assaulted Yankee positions.

Again, according to Wiley, the Trans-Mississippi Indian version of the Yell was on full display in the following two incidents: "Colonel Tandy Walker, commander of the Second Indian Brigade, reporting an action of his troops in Arkansas, said that when the Federals retreated, Private Dickson Wallace was the first man to reach their artillery, 'and mounting astride one of the guns gave a whoop, which was followed by such a succession of whoops from his comrades as made the woods reverberate for miles around.'"

The second incident is an expansion of his comments about the Indian soldiers at Wilson's Creek. At the 1861 battle in Southwest Missouri "the number of red men involved was small and their chief contribution seems to have been the rousing war whoop which they had taught to their paleface comrades. In a charge led by Colonel Greer, the savage shriek, issuing from both Choctaws and Texans, blended with the Rebel yell to create surprise, if not alarm, in Union ranks."

The following is an account by Colonel O.M. Roberts commander of the 11th Texas Infantry after engaging in several battles in Louisiana:

> The Texas soldiers in line of battle, with their attention intensely alive to what they were doing and how they should act, were cool enough and intelligent enough to pass the word along the whole line of battle like an electric current; and when the command was given, 'Forward, charge!' it, too, would be rapidly passed, and then simultaneously the Texas 'rebel yell' burst out from the whole line, as all together they dashed at double quick toward the enemy. The effect of that yell was marvelous....Such yells exploded on the air in one combined sound have been heard distinctly three miles odd across a prairie, above the din of musketry and artillery.

In the early pages of Thomas Dixon, Jr.'s 1905 novel *The Clansman* there is a scene where a Union doctor working at a hospital in Washington is describing to the book's heroine his memory of being on the receiving end of a Rebel charge at Petersburg. While coming from a work of fiction, it seems to have the power and impact of truth behind it: "There were not more than three hundred of them now, but on they came, giving that hellish rebel yell at every jump—the cry of the hunter from the hilltop at the sight of his game! All Southern men are hunters, and that cry was transformed in war into something unearthly when it came from a hundred throats in chorus and the game was human."

Since the fame of the Rebel Yell has stood up through the decades, it seems only fair to throw in a couple of more currently oriented comments: A blogger after reading an article about the Yell wrote: "I didn't need this to tell me that it was unnerving to be charged by a whole gang of Confederates screeching at the tops of their lungs. Plenty of contemporary reports from Union soldiers confirm that the sound scared 'em $#!+less."—Senator Jim Webb, writing in the *Wall Street Journal* about the importance of the Democrats winning back the Scots-Irish vote, cited the incident in which a national party leader "suggested that the Democrats needed to reach out to the 'guys with the Confederate flags on their pickup trucks.'" To which a prominent newspaper columnist wrote that the politician in question "'wants the white trash vote...' and that he is pandering to 'rebel-yelling racist rednecks.'"—Based on the preceding, maybe the Civil War isn't quite over yet!

Finally, H. Allen Smith offered this "smile inducing" little tidbit: "I would, however, like to mention Stonewall Jackson's horse. Every time the horse heard the rebel yell he went into a little cross-legged dance, as if he understood and was proud of the screeches he was hearing."—Jackson's horse, Little Sorrel, lived to age thirty-six and was buried near Jackson's statue at the Virginia Military Institute.

CHAPTER 16

Poetry: Voice of the South

While I know poetry isn't for everyone, it nonetheless is one of the basic forms of literature and consequently deserves some mention. I must confess to being a poet myself, so I probably have an affinity for appreciating and sharing poetry with others. But there are several good reasons for offering poems about the Rebel Yell besides my own interest.

First, we must remember that during the nineteenth-century poetry was much more pervasive than it is today. It was extremely popular and a common form of expression by many different classes and groups of people. Because of this factor alone, it should receive some consideration. Of course, just as with prose, the style and vocabulary of the time were very different from today's poetry.

Second, poetry has always served as an avenue for exploring emotions, feelings, and thoughts; a way of shining a light on what's inside. Ultimately, this can lead to more candor, and a purer, clearer idea of the thematic material. This is particularly true when dealing with the statistics and minutiae of a subject such as the Civil War, or specifically the Rebel Yell. The emotion can get lost in the smoke and bloody boot prints.

The poems offered below are primarily from the late 1800s and early 1900s; they were written by veterans or their relatives and many appeared in the *Confederate Veteran* magazine. Most of the poems are what might be called average in length, although one is of near epic proportions. Not surprisingly, there are some recurrent themes expressed—two of the poets finding a Yell correlation in the same biblical reference.—In addition, I've included some more recent poems about the Yell which express a current and ongoing interest. One of these poems is "found poetry," which is writing that is not intended as poetry, but which has poetic elements and when the bits and pieces are "massaged" a poem emerges.

I'm sure these are not the only poems concerning the Rebel Yell; a great many may exist that have never even seen the light of day, having spent the years tucked away somewhere with other artifacts.

Finally, I will make no comments on the nature or quality of these poems, as they need to stand on their own. Poetry is such an individual taste that critiques are generally not worthwhile anyway. I think if we keep in mind the sincerity behind them it will help overcome any literary shortfalls which may exist.

The Rebel Yell

Hear the old Confederate yell—Rebel yell!
    Once what deathly summons
    Did its acclamation tell!
How it echoed and re-echoed
    All along the charging line,
Rising higher with the clashing
Of the column's murderous flashing
    In a frenzy superfine;
Dealing death, death, death
In the passion of each breath
    That uplifted in the wild, defiant yell.

Author: Unknown
From a newspaper of 1864
Confederate Veteran Vol. 40, 1932

Untitled

The yell was different from all the sounds
Ever heard. The throats of maddened hounds
Of starved hyenas, and angry beasts

In deadly fight over bloody feasts,
Or wails of souls in purgatory.
Lost to heaven and all its glory,
Ne'er cast over man such awful spells
Of terror as did those Rebel Yells.

Author: Unknown Federal soldier
Original date unknown
The Rebel Yell Lives! 2008

The Rebel Yell

The scene we present is the army in gray
    Bivouacked where it halted from long, weary march.
Not sheltered by tents, on their blankets they lay,
    And canopied over with heaven's grand arch.

'Tis spring of the year, and flowerets are blooming—
    The features of Nature are broadening with smiles;
The winter is past, the birds are resuming
    Their carols which charm us and man's care beguiles.

The morn is just dawning, the usual sound
    Of reveille calls from the camps far and near.
At times well defined with notes full and round,
    Then fainter, like echoes, it dies on the ear.

Aroused from their sleep, the soldiers are waking
    From sleep that to some was tranquil and sweet,
While dreaming of home, and in dreams merry-making
    With those whom they longed in embraces to greet.

To others the long, weary watches of night
    Were restless and brought neither sleep nor repose.
For movements were making which told them they might
    Ere long be grappling in death with their foes.

A clatter of hoofs is heard fast approaching—
    A courier hurriedly making his rounds;

He follows no path, but on camp lines encroaching
    He urges his steed where a footing is found.

Without a delay, he reaches headquarters;
    He does not dismount, so great is his haste.
With tip of his cap he issues his orders;
    'Tis evident time is too precious to waste.

But a moment elapses—the adjutants call:
    "Form your companies!" Orderlies quickly reply,
"Fall in! Fall in, men!" Abandoning all,
    Responsive to duty, the soldiers comply.

Conveying their orders, couriers are dashing,
    And movements are rapid as columns combine;
Artillery corps at their teams wildly lashing,
    Battalions and companies wheel into line.

The lines are completed, the soldiers well know
    'Tis theirs to obey, and are ready to serve;
They await the command which shall tell them to go
    With moments of exquisite tension of nerve.

All now is made ready and waiting the word;
    Waiting—yes, waiting with feelings intense.
The signal—the boom of a cannon is heard.
    The sound's a relief from the dreadful suspense.

        Attention, Battalion!
Command given "Load," and the ring of the rammer,
    As driving the cartridge, it springs and rebounds;
The rustle of boxes, click of the hammer
    At once are suggestive and ominous sounds.

O, who can forget it that ever has heard
    The "Forward, Guide Center" which rings on the ear?
And followed by "Charge," that terrible word
    Which starts off the line in its maddening career!

As surges the waves of the tempest-tossed ocean,
    When lashed into fury by boisterous gales,
It rises and falls in ceaseless commotion,
    Then breaks on the rocks in murmurs and wails.

So move the long ranks of the fierce "line of battle"
    As onward it sweeps with disastrous flow;
It charges 'mid shot, shell, and musketry's rattle,
    And bursts in its fury when met by the foe.

Plunged into flashes of dense liquid fire,
    Facing the rain of bullets and shell,
'Mid columns of smoke mounting higher and higher,
    Regardless of fate they rush in with a yell!

Down the declivities, mounting the knolls,
    Sweeping more rapidly over the plains,
A vast living mass like a fire it rolls;
    Humanity lost, pandemonium reigns.

The roar of the cannon, the musketry fire,
    The whiz of the bullets, the shriek of the shells
Are sounds to which even the demons aspire;
    Resounding o'er all are the fierce Rebel yells.

Methinks the first time this yell was e'er given
    With reverence, we say, it was by God's command;
The order was issued directly from heaven.
    The thought is majestic, superlative, grand!

'Twas Joshua, leader of Israel's hosts,
    Who was told to compass a city about,
And follow instructions, with all at their posts.
    The people he led should smite in a shout.

Conceive, if you can, of the terror conveyed
    By this loud-swelling chorus of shouting or yell;
The hearts of strong men were with horror dismayed

As the walls of Jericho crumbled and fell.

This yell untaught is a wild inspiration
    Which comes all unbidden—a gush of the soul;
Voice of the South, it defies imitation.
    It comes in prolonged and continuous roll.

The harvest of death a wide swath is mowing,
    The dead and the dying are strewn o'er the field;
Yet steadily onward, like tidal wave flowing,
    They rush toward the goal, to no obstacle yield.

The solid earth trembles, the elements quake,
    And heaven itself with vibration is bowed.
Withdrawn from confusion which mortals can make,
    The sun has thrown over its features a cloud.

An enfilade fire of canister, raking
    From batteries in gray which have broken the flanks,
Is sweeping the works, and havoc is making
    As shots well directed pour into the ranks.

The starry cross over the breastworks is borne—
    A host to sustain it have gathered around.
Down, by a volley of bullets 'tis torn;
    Up, again floating, it springs with a bound.

Into the breastworks, commingled the flashing
    Of fire which leaps out like tongues from the gun:
Hand to hand conflict, their bayonets clashing,
    Fighting like demons, the triumph is won.

The voices which joined in these shouts years ago
    Are silent in death or by Time are subdued.
They never again so discordant can flow;
    They never can be with their vigor renewed.

May the yell of the future be shoutings of joy

Whenever exultant our voices we raise!
May the thoughts of our hearts and our lips find employ
In joyful thanksgiving and paeans of praise!

Author: Captain F. J. V. L'Cand
Confederate Veteran Vol. 15, 1907

The Rebel Yell

Long ago the Southern legion
    Sprang from every nook and dell,
Called to meet their foes advancing,
    Met them with a mighty yell.

'Twas the battle cry of freedom.
    Fast and hard flew shot and shell,
While strong throats were still repeating
    That immortal Southern yell.

Was there ever such a trumpet
    Sending forth such sounds to tell
Of glory of the fighting
    As that piercing, surging yell?

Once there was a shout more like it
    When that ancient city fell,
And the host of Joshua's army
    Felled its walls with one great yell.

'Twas the same old inspiration
    Prompting them again to tell
Of the warrior's jubilation
    When his soul was in his yell.

'Twas the yell that spurred the charging
    Of the batteries aimed so well,
Till the breath of fire and courage
    Conquered breastworks through its spell.

What the army lacked in numbers
　　Every man his lungs would swell;
And though hungry, ragged, bleeding,
　　Giant strength they gave each yell.

For beneath the Southern armor,
　　Where brave hearts and honor dwell,
Valor, pride, and faithful knighthood
　　Hold the secret of that yell.

And in spirit those old heroes
　　Would, their country's foes to quell,
Forces join with those who fought them,
　　Share with them their generous yell.

Author: Kate Coles Donegan
Confederate Veteran Vol. 22, 1914

The Rebel Yell

Send its echoes down the ages!
　　Let its martial challenge ring,
Born amid the battle's rages,
　　Soaring on exultant wing!

From Fame's battlement revealing
　　Dauntless courage to all earth,
Stern the lips that sent it pealing,
　　Pure the Cause that gave it birth.

Let it live, proclaiming loudly
　　Tramp of armies in advance
'Neath that banner streaming proudly,
　　Led by Lee's imperial glance!

Tell its story to all nations!
　　Down the trail of unborn feet,
Let it thrill new generations,
　　Still triumphant in defeat!

Where embattled hosts lie sleeping,
   Sounds the Rebel Yell no more.
Who shall say what dreams they're keeping
   Safe beyond the cannon's roar?

Pledged to conquest or death's pallor,
   Martyr's in unequal feud,
On the hallowed urn of Valor
   Gleams the tears of gratitude.

Shall the South forget? Nay, never!
   Let that clarion call resound
Immemorial endeavor
   Echoed all the world around!

Author: Lilita Lever Younge
Confederate Veteran Vol. 40, 1932

The Rebel Yell

None of us have ever heard it.
   None of us ever will.
There's no one left who can give it.
   Tho you may hear its echo still.

You may hear it up near Manassas,
   and down around Gaines Mill.
In December it echoes in Fredericksburg,
   in May around Chancellorsville.

It's the "pibroch of Southern fealty."
   It's a Comanche brave's battle cry.
It's an English huntsman's call to the hounds.
   It's a pig farmer's call to the sty.

It's a high-pitched trilling falsetto.
   It's the yip of a dog in flight.
It's the scream of a wounded panther.
   It's the shriek of the wind in the night.

It was yelled when the boys flushed a rabbit.
It was passed man to man in the ranks.
It was cheered when they saw their leaders.
It was screamed when they whipped the Yanks.

But none of us will ever hear it.
Tho some folks mimic it well.
No soul alive can truly describe
the sound of the Rebel Yell.

Author: Monte Akers
stonewallbrigade.com, 2008

Untitled Found Poetry

In the still of the night,
    as I hear the song
        of the cricket
            and tree frog
I remember Gettysburg,
    Cemetery Ridge,
        and those who fell
            at Vicksburg

On a cold, starry,
    night in Dixie
        I want to be in
            the company of
                my friends
On a cold, starry,
    night in Dixie,
        that's when I want
            to hear the
                Rebel Yell

Even though the Yell
    is now an echo,
        it still resonates
            with those

who see beyond
 the label of racism,
  and can understand
   the truth and lessons
    of heritage and history.

Authors: T. McGee and Hilltop
Found, assembled and edited by: T. Elliott
freerepublic.com, 2009

CHAPTER 17

Epilogue: Conclusions

We've had a fairly interesting journey exploring the Rebel Yell—hopefully this is true even for those of you who hate poetry and skipped the previous chapter. But now it's time to evaluate the information we've gathered, reach some conclusions and see what we can take away with us that is reasonably reliable.

On the subject of origins I believe we can safely come to several conclusions that have been adequately backed up by the facts that have been presented.

The first of these would be the Celtic influence on the Rebel Yell. The demographic numbers alone indicate the importance of this group of people, not only to the Yell but to the South in general. But in addition we've discovered a long martial history for the Celts which stretch from ancient times in Britain to the Civil War in America. That history has many correlations through the centuries including well known and feared battle cries.

Of the various Celtic peoples that have an important role in the make-up of the antebellum South and consequently the Rebel Yell, the most important are the Scots-Irish. Their history, population, geographic location and lifestyle all affirm the value of their contributions on both counts.— Without doubt the other two primary Celtic groups, the Highland Scots and the native Irish, also played a valuable role. In the case of the Highland Scots, their part in the story of the Yell cannot be underestimated.

In direct relation to the influence of the Celts, since most of them assumed this lifestyle, there is also the rural effect on the Rebel Yell. The general term "rural" covers a number of specifics which all contributed to the end product. Included would be the mountain lifestyle with its long distance hollering as a method of communication. Next would be farming, the presumptive occupation of the majority, with its various calls to the livestock. In addition, there would be the hunting aspect of rural life in its many forms. No matter what the game—fox, rabbit, coon, 'possum, deer, bear, birds or any other—hunting in the South almost invariably involved the use of dogs, and that in turn involved hollered and yelled signals, much of the time over considerably distance.

So, we have the rural lifestyle of a large population of historically militant Celtic emigrants as our first definitive piece of the puzzle.

While the Native American influence on the Rebel Yell may have had more effect in the Trans-Mississippi theater than elsewhere, I don't think we should discount its overall importance. It must be remembered that a substantial number of American Indians still lived in the Southeastern United States at the time of the Civil War.

These soldiers not only contributed their various traditional war cries directly to the Rebel Yell, but more importantly they passed them on to their white, Confederate allies. The white soldiers from Texas, Arkansas, Louisiana and Missouri then adopted the Native American war whoop into their versions of the Rebel Yell, and as the War progressed and units were transferred, this American Indian influence spread to large parts of the Confederate Army.

To realize the significance of the Native American contribution to the Yell all you need to do is look at the many writers who in some way incorporated the term "Indian war whoop," or a similar phrase, into their descriptions.

Now we come to the difficult task of trying to make sense out of what we've uncovered concerning the description and sound of the Rebel Yell. It won't be easy, but I think we can make some firm observations, as well as, some reasonable speculations.

Far too many of the descriptions we've found have, in various ways, referred to the Rebel Yell as being "high-pitched" for this quality to be ignored. Some terms, besides "high-pitched," which have been employed include "falsetto," "woman-like," "shriek," "effeminate" and "screech" among others. Plus, when some basic logic is applied to many of the other descriptive words and phrases, such as some of the various comparisons to animal sounds, it's easy to see an indirect, implied link to the high-pitched, falsetto quality of the Yell. In addition, the accepted understanding of the Native American war cry as being high-pitched in nature is another factor which gives credence to this concept.—With all this in mind, I think that we can safely conclude that this quality was true of the majority, if not all, of the various versions of the Yell.

One thing we know for certain is that there are numerous different descriptions of the Rebel Yell, both by word and phrase, and by phonetic spelling. These descriptions are literally all over the map. They vary dramatically from one another, and come from many different sources from every part of the country.

We've already discussed above the single aspect of the Yell that many of the descriptions have in common; but what of all the others?—How do we reconcile such diverse descriptions as: "A peculiar, apelike grunt"; "a foxhunt 'yip'"; "a wolf-howl"; and "a tomcat at midnight"?—In the phonetics realm we have everything from, "Wa-woo-woohoo, wa-woo-woohoo!" to "Yai, yai, yi, yai, yi!"

I believe the answer to this dilemma is that we don't even attempt to reconcile these differences. Rather, we should accept the fact that different people will hear and interpret sounds individually, and ultimately express themselves in a vast number of divergent ways. The best we can do is, using the information at hand, decide for ourselves which description or phonetic sound seems the most likely or makes the most sense. In lieu of that, we can alternatively pick out the ones we like best; the ones that make us smile or bring a gleam of recognition to our eyes.

I personally like Don Bracken's description: "An audible

sensation of being overwhelmed." It very well conveys the power and threatening nature of the Yell.—For accuracy, I prefer Kellar Anderson's a "penetrating, rasping, shrieking, blood-curdling noise." It neatly incorporates the main aspects in common with many other descriptions, plus, he was there and would have known the sound intimately.— To elicit the high-pitched nature of the Yell, I can think of no better phrase than: "squalling Banshee."

As for phonetic spelling, I'm fond of the hog-calling based, "Hooooooooooooo-eeeeeeeeeeee! Hooooooooooooo-eeeeeeeeeeee! Yip, yip, yip, yip, yip!" Mostly, I just like the sound and the fact that it comes from a definitively rural background.—Based on the recorded sound evidence, I think J. Harvie Dew's versions (Woh-who-ey! who-ey!, etc.) are remarkably close, as are others of a similar nature. Plus, he was in the right place to know the sound well. Somewhat surprisingly, I feel that another of the more acceptable phonetic versions may very well be the one in Margaret Mitchell's *Gone With the Wind*. Her simple, "Yee-aay-eee" repeated a number of times, fits quite nicely with the known sound archives. Additionally, she too would have been in a good position, in reference to time and location, to be familiar with the Yell and consequently to know what she was writing about. A few others, which are close to Mitchell's version, should also be given some consideration.

We can probably come closer to determining which of the various descriptions and phonetic versions of the Yell are not so great. Certainly there are questionable ones as well as those which are downright ludicrous.

In the word description category, I personally have never cared for the comparisons to the scream of a rabbit and the scream of an elephant. These two are pretty much on the opposite extremes size-wise in both the animal and sounds area. Somehow, in my mind, neither ever seemed to fit the concept very well; one was too small and other too large. I can go along with the idea of it being a rabbit hunter's call, but not the rabbit itself. An elephant doesn't really scream, it trumpets in an almost roaring fashion. Because the common phrase of the day, "seeing the elephant," referred to going into battle, it's possible we can attribute some of the cause for this comparison in that direction.—Other descriptions, may or may not appeal to your individual taste or view of the facts.

The list of phonetic versions has many candidates for the "worst attempt at describing the sound of the Rebel Yell" category: The "Keeook!" of the Panther Patrol, the "Eee-Yow!" from *Time* magazine, the "Yay-hoo!" from the movie version of *Gone With the Wind* and the generic "Yee-haw!" heard in many movies and television shows all come to mind. One comment concerning the last of these was that, "'Yee-haw' conveys a message of, 'Oh boy! We's gonna' have some fun now!'" Whereas, any of the more realistic versions of the Rebel Yell convey "more of an 'Oh boy! We's gonna' do some killin' now!' message....The desired effect requires an entire horde of Southerners with an extreme case of battle lust."

The most logical explanation for the large number and widely varying descriptions of the Rebel Yell is simply that there were many different versions. The Yell undoubtedly varied from theater to theater, state to state, unit to unit and even soldier to soldier. There is ample evidence to support this claim, both in contemporary accounts as well as in the opinions expressed by various experts.

H. Allen Smith, writing about Dr. Bell Irvin Wiley, said, "Dr. Wiley concedes that there were variations of the yell, that a Mississippian's screech was not like the yawp of a Virginian and that the Indians who fought for the Confederacy contributed a few vocal arpeggios to the general confusion."

Historian and author, James Street, was quoted in the *Raleigh News & Observer* as saying, "Actually, there were as many kinds of rebel yells as there were rebels."

In Virginia Beach, Virginia H. Allen Smith talked to a newspaperman, who wanted to remain anonymous, but who had a view on the Yell, as well as on the Yankee Cheer and world military history. He told Smith the following:

> The rebel yell is pure legend. In Richmond it goes one way. In Atlanta you'll hear it another. In Birmingham, still another.
>
> Throughout history, foot soldiers have always bellered their heads off during battle. The Persians yelled the rebel yell at Thermopylae and the Spartans yelled the rebel yell right back at them. The British grenadiers yelled it at Balaklava and the Russians screeched it back. The Communists in Korea yelled it at us and we didn't answer them with mumbles....
>
> I'm certain that the Yankee hordes yelled just as much as the Confederates. And they probably yelled the same kind of yell. It may be that our boys started it; but you know very well that if a wave of our boys came charging out of the woods, shrieking the rebel yell, the Yankees didn't greet them with silence. It stands to reason that the Yankee officers ordered, 'Outscreech the bastards, men!' And they probably did.

It's easy to see why this Southern journalist wanted to remain anonymous. While some aspects of his ideas on the subject seem well founded, I can't buy the whole package, particularly the final paragraph; there's too much evidence to the contrary.

Monte Akers has summed up his thoughts on the subject as follows:

> I think that different units and armies gave different versions of the Yell....All of [the various] attributions are probably correct. At the time the Yell became famous, its sponsors were simply yelling in an excited manner, the way all soldiers have yelled for time immemorial, and the yell they selected was surely the same one they used back home when they were excited. Why should they have given the exact same sound? [Lee's Army of Northern Virginia may have sounded a certain way]...but what of the Army of Tennessee, and those in the Trans-Mississippi? They were yelling long before anyone from Virginia came west to teach them how.

It's fair to say that while there may have been a dominant

Eastern theater version of the Rebel Yell; there were also many others which were heard across the battlefields of the War. With all these different Yells, it seems that the concept of multiple origins and sources is very likely.

But there is another major consideration, which until now we have only touched on briefly. Almost from the beginning of the War, and certainly as it progressed and the situation grew tighter for the South, there was a huge amount of troop movement. Units from the three major theaters of the conflict, as well as specific, smaller geographic areas, were transferred within theaters and from one theater to another as the need arose. It is inconceivable that this movement and interaction among troops from all over the Confederacy would not have had a substantial impact in many ways, one of which must have been the Rebel Yell.

The Texans learned from the Native American soldiers of the Indian Territory and then passed it along to the Rebels from Missouri and Arkansas. The Mississippi, Louisiana and Alabama units loaned their versions to soldiers of Tennessee and Georgia, Virginia and North Carolina sent their Yell south and west, and so on and so forth.

I am convinced that as this interaction occurred there was a "homogenization" of the Rebel Yell which blended many of the divergent variations and styles, so that by War's end a similar Yell could be heard on a number of different fronts. This is not to say that the classic Northern Virginia Yell couldn't be heard right up until Appomattox, or that any of the other regional versions had disappeared. Rather that this homogenized version (or versions) had joined the mix.

Next, let's address and evaluate the relatively few recorded versions of the Yell that are available.

First, while it is a shame that more recordings don't exist, since there was ample opportunity from the 1890s forward to have made additional records, we are lucky to have the ones that do exist. Unless others turn up in the future, they are all we have to make the Rebel Yell come alive again.

Second, we are extremely fortunate that numerous people through the years have taken it upon themselves to pursue these recordings, save them, embellish them and make them accessible to a wider public audience.

The CD that has been released by the Museum of the Confederacy is the current high-water mark in Rebel Yell recordings. Two individual Yells, which seem to validate one another in style, are the basis for the CD. The men involved were old at the time the recordings were made, although it doesn't appear to have affected their ability to cut loose with a strong Yell; one can only speculate how much different these two gentlemen may have sounded in their prime. The various computer enhancements lend a dramatic element to the recording which sparks the imagination.

But the question which still begs to be answered is, "which Rebel Yell are we hearing?" While the two were recorded in different years and a continent apart they do sound nearly identical. Does it mean that this version is in fact *the* Rebel Yell? We must remember that the two old veterans involved came from Virginia and North Carolina and both served in the same theater of the war. It would only be logical to assume that their Yells would be similar to one another. Once again, we have to regret that there aren't more recordings and other versions to compare them to.

So, where does this leave us? I think we can safely say that the Museum of the Confederacy CD, *The Rebel Yell Lives!*, is certainly excellent and the best sound evidence we have to date; it is our present "gold standard." Minimally, it displays what is the most classic version of the Rebel Yell, that of the Army of Northern Virginia and the Eastern theater of the Civil War. What percentage of territory it may represent beyond that, and how it differs from other versions, both regional and blended, is anyone's guess.

As mentioned earlier, it's been said that the Rebel Yell was as much a part of a Confederate soldier's equipment as his rifle and uniform. With it he could supposedly work battlefield miracles, since the Yankees, at the mere sound of the Yell, would turn tail and run, time after time.

It's possible that the power of the Rebel Yell has been embellished through the decades, first by the veterans and later by others, as it made its way from memory to legend. For one thing, we have to deal with the fact that the South lost the war. The Union Army was still standing after Gettysburg and Vicksburg, and was there to receive Lee's surrender at Appomattox. If Billy Yank ran every time that Johnny Reb cut loose with a blood-curdling Yell, how did this happen?

The obvious answer is that while the Rebel Yell was an effective weapon, the Northern soldiers didn't always turn and run. And while the Yell did at times have an impact on the battlefield, in the end it couldn't make up for a lack of manpower, food and munitions.

Ultimately, the myth may be more important than the reality!

APPENDIX A

Web Sites for Recorded Rebel Yell

As of the publication of this book, the following web sites had the listed items available for listening and viewing.

A. en.wikipedia.org/wiki/Rebel_yell (via links)
1. The Thomas Alexander 1935 recording made by WBT Radio.
2. The 1938 Gettysburg reunion newsreel.
3. Audio only version of unit in simulated battle, made from sound on newsreel.
B. www.26nc.org/History/Rebel-Yell/rebel-yell
1. The Thomas Alexander recording: Short version (11 seconds)
2. The Thomas Alexander recording: Long version (36 seconds)
C. www.historypublishingco.com/Articles
1. The Thomas Alexander recording.
2. A simulated battle version made to sound like a company charging.
D. www.youtube.com/watch/confederaterebelyell
1. Gettysburg reunion newsreel.
2. Audio only of simulated battle.
E. www.youtube.com/watch/realrebelyell
1. The Thomas Alexander recording.
2. Simulated version of a company charging.

APPENDIX B

Videos, DVDs and CDs
for Recorded Rebel Yell

As of the publication of this book, the following items could be purchased at numerous retail, mail order and internet sites, except as noted.

A. Gettysburg 1938 reunion newsreel. (Video and DVD)
   1. Ken Burns' *Civil War*—Final volume.
   2. *Echoes of the Blue and Gray*—Volume II.
B. *The Rebel Yell Lives* (CD)
   Available only from the Museum of the Confederacy at www.mocstore.org (click—Haversack Store Online Exclusives!)
   1. The Thomas Alexander recording.
   2. The Sampson Simmons recording.
   3. The Alexander and Simmons recordings blended and remixed to simulate a charge by various sized units.
      a. 70 man company
      b. 500 man regiment
      c. 1800 man brigade
      d. The Army of Northern Virginia

APPENDIX C

Graphic of Sound Analysis

The following graphic was also contributed by the author to Monte Akers' book, *The Accidental Historian, etc.*... It appears in note 9 on page 212.

Both the Alexander/WBT and the Simmons/UDC recording are 20 seconds in length. They each follow the six-part pattern illustrated below of standard short yelps...lower, gruffer short yelps...long three-part yelps...short pauses and long pauses.

Legend

 __   standard short yelp

 —   lower, gruffer short yelp

- - -   long three-part yelp

/   short pause

//   long pause

Pattern

This six-part pattern (each part separated by a short / or long // pause) is identically repeated in both the Alexander and Simmons version of the Yell. This has led to speculation that they may indeed be the same recording, with the most likely contributor being Simmons due to the provenance of that particular recording.

Sound Graphic for the Alexander Yell

__ __ --- / __ __ --- // __ __ --- / __ __ --- // __ __ --- / __
__ ---

Sound Graphic for the Simmons Yell

__ __ --- / __ __ --- // __ __ --- / __ __ --- // __ __ --- / __
__ ---

NOTES

Note 1

During the writing and research of this book I accessed every available source I could locate in order to make this as complete an account of the history of the Rebel Yell as possible. I then attempted to evaluate and, in some instances, rate the information by importance and veracity. The intent of those efforts was clarification and accuracy.

However, if errors of commission, omission or interpretation do exist, they are strictly my own and no one else's.

Note 2

At several points during the preceding text I made reference to the novel, *The Clansman*, by Thomas Dixon, Jr. As indicated, this book has achieved somewhat of a dubious reputation due to its radical views on reconstruction in the post-war South. I have included those references not in support of the views expressed, but rather for the Scots-Irish content and Rebel Yell description.

In the spirit of full disclosure I now include first, the book's sub-title and then, the text of the dedication which Thomas Dixon penned:

"AN HISTORICAL ROMANCE
OF THE KU KLUX KLAN"

"To the Memory of
A Scotch-Irish Leader of the South
My Uncle, Colonel Leroy McAfee

Grand Titan of the Invisible Empire
Ku Klux Klan

Note 3

The quote from the anonymous Virginia Beach newspaperman, which appeared in chapter 17, has been incorrectly attributed by several sources to Douglas Southall Freeman.

Note 4

During the early phases of the War in Indian Territory a mixed-blood Cherokee named Clem Rogers, who may very well have cut loose with a Rebel Yell or two, served as a scout for a Confederate unit composed primarily of Choctaw and Chickasaw warriors. Later, he had a son who gained stage, radio and film stardom—the humorist Will Rogers.

Note 5: New Information—New Questions

The following was contributed by the author to Monte Akers' 2010 book, *The Accidental Historian—Tales of Trash and Treasure*. It appears there in chapter 5, between pages 63 and 68. With Monte's permission I am including it in this edition.

One thing about the Rebel Yell—not unlike the rest of history—is that just about the time you think you're getting a handle on it along comes some new discovery or information of some sort, which then has to be taken into consideration and accounted for. And, generally speaking, this new knowledge seems to raise more questions than it answers.

This is the case with the recorded versions of the Rebel Yell. We have the excellent CD released by The Museum of the Confederacy, *The Rebel Yell Lives!*, which incorporates the Alexander/WBT recording and the Simmons/UDC recording along with several enhanced versions to simulate increasingly larger units. All of this appeared to be on solid footing, and indeed might have been the final word. After all, the two were so similar to one another that they each appeared to corroborate the sound and authenticity of the other. Plus, the provenance for each recording was apparently spotless. But now some new, or at least previously uncirculated, information has surfaced that is causing some concern and questions.

Based on communications recently with Waite Rawls and John Coski at The Museum of the Confederacy (they are the President and Historian respectively and the folks responsible for the Rebel Yell CD) and also with Clint Johnson a Civil War author, historian and reenactor with the 26th North Carolina (he was one of the people initially involved in bringing the Alexander recording to light and putting it on the 26th N.C. site) this is how I piece the story and situation together:

Clint Johnson and Ken Curtis (a fellow reenactor) became aware of the recording of Alexander from his grandson, J.B. Joye, about 2002.—The family story was that at some point after the recording was made in 1935 a request was made to WBT for a copy which was furnished to them on some medium (possibly a record or some type of reel-to-reel recording). This was eventually transferred to a cassette tape, which is what J.B. Joye possessed.—Johnson and Curtis received Joye's permission to copy it and post it on their website. There were three parts to the recording: An interview with Alexander, a Rebel Yell by a group of old veterans and Alexander's solo Yell. According to Clint, at that time there was no MP3, and digital recording was difficult to do and post, so the decision was made to post only the solo Yell. At that point there was some rumored knowledge of the other two parts, but most people (myself included) hadn't ever heard them and didn't know if they actually existed.

As time went by, the solo version of the Yell spread to various locations on the web and finally the folks at the MOC got it and started a proactive approach to enhance and disseminate it, eventually resulting in their CD. Of course, as previously stated, the CD also included the Simmons/ UDC solo recording of the Yell. There's no need to go into the whole story again here, but suffice it to say that Waite Rawls had all he could handle prying the recording from the well-meaning grasp of the ladies at the UDC.

Rawls and Coski were elated to have the "confirming" Simmons recording and, as indicated, proceeded with the production of the CD. In the year or so since its release their initial elation has been tempered by a gnawing concern: The two versions of the Yell were almost *too* similar! Some fairly elementary audio testing was conducted and it was discovered that each recording was exactly 20 seconds in length. In addition, both are comprised of a repeating pattern of the "yelp" which makes up the total Yell. Each pattern has two short yelps followed by a longer yelp, which has three secondary parts to it. This pattern is repeated six times in each recording. Furthermore, there are slight variations during the repeated patterns. Between patterns two and three and patterns four and five there is a slightly longer pause than between the other patterns. Also, four of the short yelps have a lower and slightly gruffer quality to them. The point of interest here is that each of these variations occurs identically in both recordings. The implication here is fairly obvious: The two recordings may be one in the same!

When the recordings of the Alexander interview and the veteran's group Yell became more widely known and readily available because of digital technology, some new concerns were added to the mix. The Alexander interview reveals a fairly spry and somewhat feisty old gentleman, particularly for someone in his nineties, but without a very strong voice. The group Yell is somewhat reminiscent of the Rebel Yell on the newsreel film of the veterans at the Gettysburg reunion; it sounds a little weak and feeble. This, in turn, has led to a new suspicion about the Alexander recording. If his voice, which is so strong on the solo recording, is among those on the group recording, why isn't it more apparent? When this is coupled with the great similarity between the two recordings, the possibility is furthered that they might, in fact, be the same recording.

The Simmons/UDC recording was made in 1934 and the Alexander/WBT recording was made in 1935. The interview and group Yell recording had the Alexander solo Yell spliced onto the end of it. This could be explained in either of two ways: The solo recording was made at a different time and place and thus had to be spliced on later, or possibly the Simmons recording, for some unknown reason, at some unknown point in time, was spliced onto the end and through the years this fact was lost.

There are dozens of potential scenarios that could be proposed to clarify and/or explain these problems, some more dubious and some more likely than others. Some might even raise new questions. Consider the following: What if Alexander didn't join in with his fellow veterans during the group Yell recording? (Maybe he said something like, "That wasn't very good. Take me and your machine to another room and I'll show you how the Rebel Yell really sounded.")—What if the Alexander recording was made earlier in 1929 or 1932, as some sources suggest? Furthermore, what if Simmons, as head of the California Division of The United Confederate Veterans, was aware of the Alexander recording and rather than making a new recording in 1934 he merely acquired a copy of the earlier recording and furnished it to the movie studio?—What if there is the possibility that the "Hollywood-made" Simmons recording could have been enhanced by the studio at time it was made?—Certainly this case could have many more "what-ifs."

Another interesting point concerning the authenticity of this version of the Rebel Yell, wherever and from whomever it may have originated, is testimony from many reenactors who have switched to this form of the Yell. Waite Rawls, John Coski, and Clint Johnson all assure me that the "modern Confederates" all report that they found it easier to do on the double-quick run than what they had been doing previously.

The best we can do at this point is to appreciate, even treasure, what recorded history of the Rebel Yell we now have available and let any future "audio forensic analysis" sort out the details.—After all, half of the joy of history is speculating about the unknown aspects of it!

(See appendix C for a simple graphic analysis.)

SELECTED BIBLIOGRAPHY

Books

Bierce, Ambrose. Edited and with an introduction by McCann, William. *Ambrose Bierce's Civil War*. Wings Books, New York, NY, 1996.

Castel, Albert and Goodrich, Thomas. *Bloody Bill Anderson: The Short, Savage Life of a Civil War Guerrilla*. Stackpole Books, Mechanicsburg, PA, 1998.

Commager, Dr. Henry Steele. *The Blue and the Gray*. Bobbs-Merrill Co., Indianapolis, IN, 1950.

Cottrell, Steve. *Civil War in the Indian Territory*. Pelican Publishing Co., Gretna, LA, 1998.

Davis, Clyde Brion. *"The Great American Novel~~"*. Farrar and Rinehart, Inc., New York, NY, 1938.

Davis, William C. Technical advisor: Pritchard, Russ A. *The Fighting Men of the Civil War*. Smithmark Publishers, New York, NY, 1989.

Dixon, Thomas, Jr. *The Clansman: An Historical Romance of the Ku Klux Klan*. Grosset and Dunlap, New York, NY, 1905.

Elliott, Terryl W. *Creek Country: A True Story of Outlaws, Mayhem and Justice*. Partisan Press, Independence, MO, 2006.

Goodrich, Thomas. *Black Flag: Guerrilla Warfare on the Western Border, 1861-1865*. Indiana University Press, Bloomington, IN, 1995.

Gragg, Rod. *The Illustrated Confederate Reader*. Harper & Row Publishers, New York, NY, 1989.

Hale, Donald R. *The Life and Times of Capt. William T. Anderson, "Bloody Bill"*. Donald R. Hale, Lee's Summit, MO, revised 1998.

Hill, J.M. *Celtic Warfare 1595-1763*. John Donald Publishers Ltd., Edinburgh, Scotland, 1986.

Horowitz, Tony. *Confederates in the Attic*. Pantheon Books, New York, NY, 1998.

Johnston, David E. *The Story of a Confederate Boy in the Civil War*. Glass and Prudhomme Co., Portland, OR, 1914.

Kennedy, Billy. *The Scots-Irish in the Carolinas*. Causway Press, Greenville, SC, 1997.

Leyburn, James G. *The Scotch-Irish: A Social History*. University of North Carolina Press, Chapel Hill, NC, 1962.

MacLeod, J. *Highlanders–A History of the Gaels*. Hodder & Stoughton, London, England, 1996.

McWhiney, Grady. *Cracker Culture: Celtic Ways in the Old South*. University of Alabama Press, Tuscaloosa, AL, 1988.

McWhiney, Grady and Jamieson, Perry D. *Attack and Die: Civil War Military Tactics and the Southern Heritage*. University of Alabama Press, Tuscaloosa, AL, 1982.

Piston, William Garrett and Hatcher, Richard W. III. *Wilson's Creek: The Second battle of the Civil War and the Men Who Fought It*. University of North Carolina Press, Chapel Hill, NC, 2000.

Russell, W.H. *My Diary North and South*. T.O.H.P. Burnham Co., Boston, MA, 1863.

Smith, H. Allen. *The Rebel Yell: Being a Carpetbaggers Attempt to Establish the Truth Concerning the Screech of the Confederate Soldier Plus Lesser Matters Appertaining to the Peculiar Habits of the South*. Doubleday and Co., Garden City, NY, 1954.

Tolbert, Frank X. *An Informal History of Texas: From Cabeza de Vaca to Temple Houston*. Harper and Brothers Publishers, New York, NY, 1961.

Webb, James. *Born Fighting: How the Scots-Irish Shaped America*. Broadway Books, New York, NY, 2004.

Wellman, Paul I. *The Blazing Southwest: The Pioneer Story of the American Southwest*. W. Foulsham and Co., New York, NY, 1961.

Wiley, Dr. Bell Irvin. *The Life of Johnny Reb*. Bobbs-Merrill Co., Indianapolis, IN, 1943.

Magazines and Newspapers

Century Illustrated Magazine. Dew, Colonel J. Harvie. "The Rebel and Yankee Yells." Issue for April, 1892.

Civil War News (magazine). Boyd, Scott C. "Forget The 'Yee-haw': Capturing The Real, True, Accurate, Historical Rebel Yell." Issue for April, 2009.

Civil War Times Illustrated (magazine). Gragg, Rod. "Southern Soldiers Tales." Issue for October, 1988.

Confederate Veteran (magazine). (See below)

Anderson, Col. Kellar. "The Rebel Yell." (Republished from the *Confederate Veteran of April*, 1893.) Vol. XIII, pp. 500-501, 1905.

Anonymous. "The Rebel Yell." (Republished from a newspaper of 1864.) Vol. XL, p. 84, 1932.

Dew, J. Harvey (sic), M.D. "The Rebel and Yankee Yells." Vol. XVIX, pp. 521-522, 1911.

Donegan, Kate Coles. "The Rebel Yell." Vol. XXII, p. 98a, 1914.

Hunter, Alexander. "The Rebel Yell." Vol. XXI, pp. 218-219, 1913.

L'Cand, Capt. F.J.V. "The Rebel Yell." Vol. XV, pp. 418-419, 1907.

Love, W.A. "The So-Called Rebel Yell." Vol. XXXV, p. 445, 1927.

Morris, Wm. H. "Ohio Veteran Doesn't Like The 'Rebel Yell.'" Vol. XVIII, pp. 61-62, 1910.

Nelson, H.K. "The Last 'Rebel Yell.'" Vol. XIII, pp. 250-251, 1905.

Younge, Lilita Lever. "The Rebel Yell." Vol. XL, p. 373, 1932.

Continuity (magazine). McWhiney, Grady. "Continuity in Celtic Warfare." Vol. 2, pp. 1-18, 1981.

Journal of Southern History (magazine). McDonald, Forrest and McWhiney, Grady. "The Antebellum Southern Herdsman: A Reinterpretation." Vol. 41, pp. 147-166, 1975.

The Morning Call (newspaper). Laurel, MS, Tuesday, July 12, 1929.

The New York Times (newspaper). New York, NY, February, 1892.

Parade (magazine). Webb, James. "Why You Need to Know the Scots-Irish." Issue for October, 2004.

Web Sites

en.wikipedia.org/wiki/ (See below)
  Hillbilly
  Jubal_Anderson_Early
  Pibroch
  Rapparee
  Rebel_yell
  Scots-Irish_American
  Stand_Watie
  Stonewall_Jackson
www.9thvirginia.com/ (See below)
  coh
  rebel_yell
www.26nc.org/History/Rebel-Yell/rebel-yell
www.albanach.org/ulster
www.everything2.com/title/Rebel%2520Yell
www.freerepublic.com/focus/f-news/1432721/posts
www.history-sites.com/cgi-bin/bbs53x/mscwmb/ webbbs_config.pl?noframes;
www.home.freeuk.net/gazkhan/rebelyell
www.imbd.com/title/tt0025607/ (See below)
  maindetails
  plotsummary
  usercomments
www.listlva.lib.va.us/cgi-bin/wa.exe?A2= ind0904&L=VA-HIST&P=7284
www.members.aol.com/ha4texas/yell
www.opinionjournal.com/extra/?id=110005798
www.people.virginia.edu/~mgf2j/irish
www.stonewallbrigade.com/articles_rebelyell
www.ulsterancestry.com/ulster-scots
www.wisegeek.com/what-is-the-rebel-yell

Miscellaneous

The Rebel Yell Lives. Rawls, S. Waite III. "Rebel Yell Script." Museum of the Confederacy, 2008.

INDEX